CONSTANTINE M DHONAU

COLLATERAL INTENTIONS

A MEMOIR OF POETRY//SHORT STORIES// JOURNAL ENTRIES//LETTERS

This book is dedicated to the hearts of the many, the searching, longing, and those wilder ones. To those who seek to know their hearts and the hearts of others. To you, and to us, may we come together through aberration to find solace in solidarity of our mistakes and the gold of their lessons//

UNLOCK
ANOTHER DOOR

Who you are when you write
is written for you to see.

.ruminandum.

//Navigant

//Porro Gubernaculis

//Porro Gubernaculis

//Porro Gubernaculis

//apropos allegories //bonafide bangers //clandestine colloquialisms //desirable dissertations //eloquent entries //fascinating fillers //gripping gabs //hellenistic hits //impeccable inscriptions //jolly jokes //kingly kens //luscious lexicon //moving manuscripts //neat notes //okay orations //palatable pontifications //quintessential quotes //rude ramblings //sultry selections //tantalizing tropes //undeniable utterances //veritable vexations //wise words //exceptional xerographies //yes yodels //zesty zingers

//The following is a

com·pi·la·tion
/kämpə'lāSH(ə)n/
noun
a thing, especially a book, record, or broadcast program, that is put together by
assembling previously separate items

of

journal entries
phone notes
miscellaneous sticky notes
backs of [important] documents
paper towels
scribbled debris

col·lect·ed
/kə'lektəd/
adjective
(of individual works) brought together in one volume or edition

over eleven years;

ages

seventeen to twenty-eight.

You know, I never really get too involved. I seem to always keep a safe distance from things. Never fully commit.

I also seem to be ever-searching for role models. For idols. For heroes. For strength in others I take for lacking in my own.

I've learned the meaning of, "I apply my personality in a paste."

I am very talented at turning bad into good. My impulsiveness takes me places. Not always good. Not always bad.

Am I a complainer? I don't think so. I believe I share my troubles in a healthy and respectable way, as well as my accomplishments. I keep a balanced, natural flow. Going with the flow is good, but it's also good to know where the flow is going.

Consistently keeping a safe distance isn't a bad thing, though. It could indicate a sense of responsibility and selectivity with what one lends their passion to. Wildly surrendering deep commitment all about is a burning strain. It seems almost irresponsible, though (easily) admirable. I think many irresponsible things are admirable. "I really admire _____ for what they're doing...I know I could never do it."

What does it mean to be...idk...something big and impressive, paradoxical would be alright but expected and overplayed in this instance, which waters-down the gravity of the insight. Simple would be preferred, truly alternative in perspective (at least to the ones involved). Something so simple and beautifully re-viewed it strikes everyone with a strong, "Wow! How could I have never seen it that way before?" Something so obvious it pops-up everywhere in sight and sound, in touch and all of the senses, constantly resurfacing unignorably such that it truly does offer a lasting new perspective on one, some, many, everything, life; not just to serve the narrow moment of the conversation and create a superficial cloud of pondering; something that utters, "You know what? I'm gonna take a couple of days on that one," (as if it were a choice). This country (world? whathaveyou) is stamping out love and passion with drugs and institutions.

Fuck.

That.

.intrabit.

Volume I/

Composition

07312009 //
05032010

Ages 17 - 18

07312009

When I genuinely like a girl, I'm not clever anymore. I'm not smooth or witty. I try to muster the same slick lines and mastery and fluency that I can normally play out on the other girls - but I just make an ass of myself.
03:48 AM

08012009

I. What if we can have spiritual abnormalities? There are physical, mental, why not spiritual as well?

II. Oh please, by all means, share your deepest thoughts and opinions on existence, the state of existence, and the goings-on of existence, asshole! You're just so goddamn smart, aren't you?!? You just fucking know everything. The most ingenious motherfucker to ever grace this fucking planet. You are just so goddamn original and unique and special and attractive and deep and charming and perceptive MOTHERFUCKER. Who wouldn't want to be like you? ASSHOLE.
00:59 AM

III. This book would have to be my only installment. If I have a shitload of these then I'm never going to look through them later. I mean, if I just keep doing this, book after book, it will get boring, routine. It will just fall in as something I take for granted instead of something unique.

IV. I just wish I could see me through her eyes. She made me - MADE me. For her to think, "Wow, that came out of me…a living, functioning being, doing the things he does. It must be unbelievably rewarding just to see me alive, much less doing anything even slightly impressive. I get it now. All moms over-hype their kids like that because its amazing to them that they created life, a life that can do things with their talents, TALENTS! They made something that has a talent! Incredible…it truly is.

V. Poetry has been hitting me in waves and God are these waves beautiful. It's gotta be that bathroom. I think of some crazy shit in there. It's like a think tank.

08032009

Who's making the wrong choice? She could be making the wrong choice of guys but I could be making the wrong choice of not trying harder…DO I EVEN HAVE A CHANCE?! FUCK! I have no idea…
18:37 PM

08032009

You wrote this on a day—Wednesday—seven slash twenty-nine slash oh-nine. You were 17 years old. Questioning whether or not [she] was still interested. It seemed to bottom-out but you felt like maybe she still did, it was an odd feeling. That was kind of a weird night for you. You had Channel 16 on the

1

TV for 6+ hours because it was soothing static. You were heavily debating whether you wanted to read all of this over the phone to [her] or let her read it herself. You're a weird kid, just so you know.

Indignance
10162009

I can't stand the people
All the greed
All the malice
It's poisoning me
It's blinding me
Keeping me from who I could be

I need time away
To wash away
This slime
This sludge
It covers
It coats
It conceals
It keeps
The good in me
From shining through

What is true?
Where's the good?
Where's the God?
I'm dying inside
I'm losing life
Becoming numb

Miscellaneous Philosophies
10272009 (12312008)

> Never underestimate the healing power of good conversation.

> Don't live <u>down</u> to your stereotypes.

Social Formalities

I don't want to get a job, go to college, get a car, fall into place in society and "contribute" the way everyone else does. Our country is overly privileged and *the* world power. Our people don't need help. The countries we are ignoring and the countries we are trampling on to get what we want are the ones that need help. I want to do what I can for the people living in those countries. The American definition of "success" is material: having a car, house, steady job, large family, a college degree. My definition of success is doing what one can to help people in the world who need it most. I simply don't care to participate in the social formalities; the rite of passage growing-up in America.

I want to help people, people in deprived and warring countries who really need it. I don't want to get a job or go to college or participate in any of the other formalities of society because I don't want to have to work harder just to be unhappy like everyone else in this country. While I say I want to help these people; by not wanting to "do what it takes" (social formalities) to get there, it makes me question if I really want to help them so badly. I realize that - to me - helping those in the world who need it most is the most good a person can do in their life. Where there is a god, an afterlife, or some greater scheme to life. Helping those who need it most is the most good you can do.

Wavelength Philosophy

Life occurs across what can be described as a wavelength; more specifically, a pattern of ups and downs lasting over different lengths of time and varying highs and lows. As good as a person's life may be, their life will inevitably reach a low. There is not a set amount of low points in any person's life, but it is certain they will occur and most likely more than once. The same goes for a person in a slump, eventually, their life will pick back up onto the positive side of the wavelength. There is no way to predict how high or how low these curves will go. Everyone's baselines are also at different levels, so their lows and highs can start from different points. One person's high point might be another's low (even if they are both the same distance from their respective baselines). A high or low point may last different lengths of time as well. There is no telling when a high will fall into a low or a low build to a high.

Scope Philosophy

"Life is what you make it."
It's all in how you look at it. Say you're looking at a picture on a computer, if you zoom in you can see every little imperfection, a jumble of pixels. If you look at it in standard view it's a beautiful image. There might be an imperfection here and there, but that's what makes it so beautiful altogether. Now, if you were to try and zoom in real close to those imperfections and fix

4

them, the image would become distorted. If you zoom all the way out, the image looks like a tiny little square and you can't see the beauty of it.

The image is life, and the imperfections are your problems. If you zoom in too far, all you'll see are problems and you won't realize how beautiful it is. If you zoom out too far, you'll see life from beginning to end, the picture in its entirety, so small and minuscule that it doesn't matter. It doesn't hold any beauty or value - as small as a single pixel. You're born, then you die, what's the beauty in that? It's about finding the right scope so you can see the good and the bad collaborating together to create the masterpiece.

The Self-Serving Nature of Humans and Life

All beings live to serve themselves. Everything we do can be traced back to the motivation to better our own situation.

My Purpose in Life

Maybe my purpose in life is to be the person they can count on; that one person that no matter what will always be a shoulder to cry on, an open ear, a well of advice and a source of blunt truth and honesty.

Death

Death is not a loss, but a finality to a contribution, the release of a purpose served, therefore: a happy sacrifice.

Most Things Happen for a Reason

I once thought everything happens for a reason, but perhaps not *everything*. I don't believe such superlatives can be applied. There are some things that seem small, but given time, a moment can send ripples.

12142009

The Meaning of life is to give life meaning.

03152010

You may not be able to change the world, but you can make a difference in one person's life at a time.

03162010

It can be just as scary knowing and planning your future as not knowing.

Lost in Lust
11052009

Will she ever feel the same about me?

And with every situation
I make a relation
To my station
With her
These thoughts are
Breaking through my
Mental barriers

Will I ever be able to tell her how I feel?

I'm trying to block out
What hurts
But with every
Scenario
When I see a movie
A TV show or
Hear a song
She laces through my mind
Bound up in a rat's nest

How many nights have I gone to bed thinking and wondering about her?

Can't escape her
Can't evade her
Can't erase her
Can't replace her

Will she ever understand?

Hope it all works out
In my favor

If I am in her nightmares, at least she'll be thinking of me

Anger
06152010

Muscles tightening
Relaxation unwinding
Heat is rising
Anger is blinding

The stress is unbelievable
Pressure is inconceivable
Can't stand it
Want to scream
Need to be alone
Blow off some steam

Got to breathe
Breathe out the hate
Have no choice
But to alleviate

The hate inside
Is wounding me
Blinding me

Facade
05032010

As we grow
We draw lines around
What we know
We learn to differentiate
Between what's real and what's
fake

The facts that we get straight
For granted are what we take
We swallow what we're served
So we get what we deserve
We can't make up our own minds
So we stand in our according lines

[CHORUS]
Facade
The real world isn't real
Facade
We don't say what we really feel
Facade
We all just put a smile on
Facade
Unoffensive
And full of charm

As we live another year
The picture's supposed to
Become more clear
But with a year of hindsight
The picture doesn't seem as bright

As I practice please politely
For the foes who plot to fight me
I can't remember who I am
My mirror is a trash can

[CHORUS]

I see this life is not a dream
It's only full of misery
Deeply-seated is my hatred
For the blood and the tears shed
To perpetuate politeness
In place of open-mindedness

[CHORUS]

[BREAKDOWN]

I wish everyone would
Get the fuck away
But my need for companionship
Puts that at bay
I don't question this reality
I question those that surround me

[CHORUS x2]

[OUTRO]

Reflections on Volume I

"Composition" follows me from 17 to 19 years old in 2009 and 2010. This is when I was initiated into my journaling journey. These years were rife with hormones, lust confused for love, and lust lost. If some of these pieces made you writhe in reflection of your own adolescent angst, buckle up buttercup.

As with most things, it all started with a girl. It seemed like our crazies matched and our weirdnesses complemented each other. I was struck with inspiration to start scrawling my inner world one night, lying on the floor of her hurricane-organized room. Blue light on. Amongst the erratic system of memorabilia strewn across her dwelling, I started picking up composition books–journals–a dozen of them written in at random and kept in the same order as the rest of her life. I may have been in love. A month later her lost lover returned after a year hiatus to sweep her off her feet once more. She left me with a glitter bouncy ball, note taped to it (likely an inside joke we developed that I can't remember now), ding-dong-ditched at my door. I didn't take it personally. It was fresh enough that I accepted it as a passing fancy—less than two months—of what could have been and promptly dove into writing my every musing down for the next several years.

This took place during what some may distastefully refer to as a "grudge" with another girl. I would argue that you can't hate what isn't there. She was dead to me. Try as I might to take the higher path, my heart felt it best not to acknowledge her existence for two years. What's a guy to do? I had the opportunity to do so almost daily as I spent the bulk of my time with my best friend, who also happened to be her brother. She helped me to understand betrayal, a gift I later repaid in ways unbeknownst to her. Once I knew satisfaction, she was resurrected the following morning from the runoff of my cold shoulder, thawed overnight by the comforting flame of revenge, which leads me to back to my thesis: love lost in lust.

Towards the end of this chapter in my life, I met my first love, one that would leave a mark in an all-too-unpleasant way. Things happened fast. Her mother kicked her out of the house (again), and I welcomed her into my room (in my mom's house). We dropped the "L" bomb on each other in that first month. Halfway through the relationship, I gave her the ultimatum that if she wanted to continue stripping and overdosing in my arms, then she would need to find another boyfriend. Come six months, she cheated on me on Valentine's Day. I broke up with her. I struggled to hold my own boundary and kept coming back. She got pregnant with him. They ran off together selling meat out of a truck with a traveling circus fair. More on this later.

Enough about the girls, though. Back to what every teenager thinks they understand: myself. There were fantastic events, too. I fumbled my way into becoming the frontman for that same best friend's punk/ska band: H1N1 (formerly the Sellouts of Ska) when their frontman quit because of his girlfriend (lots of everyone having girlfriend problems). My friend slammed the car door upon his return, looked at me in the backseat, and asked, "So, you wanna join a band?" I spent the seven-hour drive to the show rehearsing every song and forgot everything in front of our enamored audience of four people shooting pool. The show organizers were nowhere to be found. We believed they were likely too high on meth to remember. These were some of the best three years of my life. I discovered an outlet for my seemingly limitless rage and inversely limited ability to regulate it. When you're on stage with a microphone, you're untouchable. I commanded my power and presence. Every practice, every performance, I screamed myself hoarse, sweated into my eyes until I couldn't see anything, stripped to my underwear, and thrashed my body into others in solidarity of our confused discontent.

This also catalyzed my formal departure from childhood, when we went on mini-tours or road trips to attend bigger festivals, and my mother had several panic attacks about her baby leaving the county or state without an "adult." I got my first job that wasn't as a summer camp counselor. I got my first car for $500 (RIP Franky: shit-brown, 1988 Toyota Camry, later sold for $600), which was the equivalent of less than two monthly car insurance payments. I started attending parties. I started throwing parties. I started experimenting with the low-key, business-as-usual substances, which I got opportunities to see again in the early morning on the floor, my clothes, or—if I was lucky—in the toilet. At long last, I was a full-blown teenager. Oh, did I mention my strained relationship with my father which led me to stop responding to his emails from Greece? More on this later.

Although I had many reasons to build and burn an effigy of what I was learning about the pain of love and relationships, I had enough positive influences in my life to offer me alternatives and challenge those beliefs. The ska community emphasized something which already had roots in my upbringing and worldview, its primary subcultural value and maxim: unity. I was educated by the community about LGBTQ+ issues, racial inequality, politics, and the unending bi-partisan debate between Streetlight Manifesto or Catch-22 (obviously Catch is superior, you cretins).

I found love and belonging for the first time. I found power in my voice and cathartic release. I found heartbreak and so set the stage for later heart-healing. I found mental stimulation and challenge. When my teen years opened with the sapling of an ego, I began to contemplate deeper meaning in my life, in the world around me, in existence itself. In these critical years, when we can be considered a "legal adult" for the first time, I grappled for my independence and freedom.

> It's not about finding a label
> It's about making your own
> This day and age
> If it's not new
> It's old//

Volume /II/

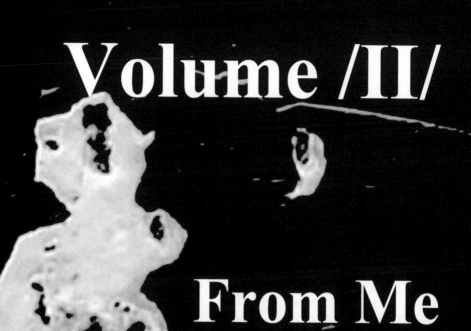

From Me
to You

10092010 // 12312011
Ages 19 - 20

A Scratched Lens
10092010

My sight limited to the surface area of two pupils
Macroscopic tunnels

Through tethering telescopes
Bountiful beauty beseeches
Beguiling
Bewildering

Blinding

Faltering focus forces frames forthwith
Endorsing elegant enclosures engrosses...enlarges
Monstrous magnification minimizes me

The world is perceived larger around me
Have I shrunk?
Yes
As my glance dances across curved lenses it
Twists
My world upside-down, obligating the brain
To toil tirelessly at topsy-turvying its tantalizations

Gaze grapples a genial and garish garden
But lo! A massacre upon these lenses upon
No! No! No!
What's this?
Sobs sound the skids
Violence violates vehemently
Scratches! Scratches! Scratches!
Be gone bifocals! Wretched readers! Cursed contacts!
Wincing wins wholesome warmth with willful withdraw
Perception previously presumed polished to perfection
provides penniless pictures, prostrated

I cannot unsee

Boundless
10212010

Bind not thy Happiness to thy self
Bind not thy Happiness to thy mother
Bind not thy Happiness to thy father
Bind not thy Happiness to all others
Bind not thy Happiness to one other
Bind not thyself to Happiness
For Happiness binds not itself to thee
Bind not Happiness whatsoever
And thy Happiness will be boundless

Pain is a Problem Making Itself Known to You
03242011

I see you crying
From the inside out
My hands are reaching for you
Ever far away

Your walls of pride and fear
Build higher by the day
My hands are bleeding
Gripping cracks in the decay

Shouting out for someone's help
From the inside
Lord knows I've tried

You won't face what lies inside of
you
For the sake of losing face outside
of you

I built a mirror of truth
As high as your wall
Your pride's defense
Went and smashed it all

All that's left
Is to walk away
A path that turns me back
Every day

Set me free from you
Haunt me no longer
All I wanted to do
Was be your savior

I wish I could show you
The cause of your unhappiness
I know the roots
Of your discontent

I see through you
I know the reasons you cry
I know how hard you try to be
Who you want to be
But that's not the person
Waiting to be free

Let it out
Let it go
Let everything show
Let everyone know

Look within
Let me in
Face your sin
Let's begin anew

To be true
To be you
To be free
To be happy

Bury no more
Run no more
Blame no more
Hate no more

Whisper Your Love so It Can Only be Heard Very, Very Close
04102011

Caught-up in the way I used to feel
This apathy
Enraptures me
Wishing I could find something real
Hoping endlessly
Tearing inside of me

All the things I could have said
Talking to myself in bed
Waiting for my wounds
To turn to scar tissue
The heart that I had
Somewhere out there with you

Give me myself back
I'm beaten blue and black
Throw my body at the ground
Kick me while I'm down

What would I say to you now?
Would you come back somehow?
I think I gave too much
And now you've got it all

Give it back
Give me back everything that I gave
I have no pieces to pick up
Since you ran away with them
And never looked back

It's Only Natural to be Wanted
09292011

Ever since the day it ended
I've been having doubts
'Bout myself
My intentions
My feelings coming out

Did I really have love for her?
Or did I just love getting into the
center of her?
Either way
I was spellbound
That's without a doubt
Hoping, wishing on her potential
The good blasted out loud
While the bad was rubbed out
But still rubbed-off
I got lost when she became a part of
me

I engrained all the pain on the
surface of my heart
Not to forget all those feelings
That burst from my heart
And from the start
I was amazed I had this power in
me
Felt so strong from being weak
around someone close to me

But now I see
All the lies
The shit she was doing on the side
The love was on one side
The other preoccupied

With demons
With running and screaming and
being a heathen
And dreaming
With tears streaming as nightmares
were revealing

The darkness she was running from
Never learned to knuckle-up
Hiding in serial love
So I stood strong and bit through
Everything she put me through

The girl I dreamed about spending
the rest of my life with

The girl to which I smiled when she
said,
"I think we have a child"
The girl I gave my heart to and took
it stripping on the pole
The girl I held in my arms through
a panic attack and withdrawals

That was really because she did a
bad line of coke-crack behind my
back
And got pissed when I called and
the ambulance showed
Made me promise not to call
because she had a guilty conscience

How many times
Did I go back on my word?
Just to satisfy a girl who is deeply
disturbed?
How naïve
I fucked myself up over a teenage
girl

Now the wounds are trying to heal
While I'm picking at the scabs
Now my heart is encrusted
With a puss-infected mustard

And I've wondered
How long before my wounded heart
fully heals
But I've trusted
In the day when my skin will peel
I've had my doubts since that day
But I'll find a new deal

16

Déjà Vu
09292011

Where am I?
What's in front of me?
Is this my face?
What do I look like inside?
How do I seem from the outside?

No ambition to play the game
No desire to get played by the
others
I won't give if I don't get back
I don't want anything
If I can't call it my own

What are these thoughts?
What is the face in the glass?
How did this happen?
Where is here?

I'm lost
It looks like I'm lost
I don't know where the fuck I am
Or where I'm going

Am I coming or going?
Moving at all?
I wonder through days over my feet
I remember things that happened
Were they yesterday?
When was yesterday?

A second passed, but I was just
there
I can remember it as if I was there
What is this barrier of time that
binds my consciousness?
Focusing my attention so narrowly
on a single moment
And shoved into the next

Not moving toward the future or
back to the past
Stuck in an instant, to an instant
One prison to the next
Wall after wall confining me in this
imprisoning moment
With a window to the past-faded
memory

And another opposite that's called
imagining
Both windows are distorted by the
windows succeeding them
The panes of memory are many

Distorting over the innumerable
series of them
Through cells and cells and cells of
moments behind
Imagining is tinted black
Such that I can't even see what my
next cell will look like
A satirical, mocking window that's
purely symbolic

Sometimes when I sleep
The walls of my prison fall away
I dance in prisons of old
Those familiar ones
The ones that seem closer than the
others
No matter how many pass between
Sometimes they're good
Sometimes bad
I only sometimes visit them

Most times, I make all new places
Without walls or windows
Big, open places
Where anything can happen
I make them out of things from my
old cells
But it's all my creation
Completely new

Every once in a while
I get pulled past that tinted window
Every so often
I see little pieces of the cells I
haven't been to yet
They're often strange to me, though
Maybe because I don't recognize
them
And I don't know where they're
from
Until I see them again
When I'm awake

Then I wake up
I'm back in a box
Moving from one to the next
Never knowing where I'm going
(but always going there)
Only where I am
And where I've been

In Response to Sonny's Blues
09302011

My head split wide open for a long moment. The edge of relief cut into my crown as if it had to sink slowly, all the way through my brain to cut every single nerve ending that created pain in me. It was like the short sting of ripping a band-aid off - but this sting was explosive pressure. I felt the salt on my face and snot on my palate, wiping off what I could of it on my clothes. The air came in short, hard gasps - more making noise than resuscitating - and my face was painted with it, twisted in such an impossible way, the muscles sucked as much blood as possible from my brain in an effort to express my anguish and joy. In an epileptic fit, overflowing joy and pulverizing torment tore through me all at once. My emotions contorted in a dance with outer struggle. Such beautiful expression, such disgusting realities it faced me with. The tears finally came. The dam that stood between inside and out had tiny faults in it, and these faults grew to cracks, and these cracks grew to fractures, until all in a blitzing hammer, the current behind slammed through, reducing the wall to chunks tossed about in a torrent like styrofoam.

God, how it stung. Needles pushed into the back of my eyes until they were full and the pings spread across my face. My sight blurred and my eyes nearly swelled out of their sockets. I thought about my father and my mother, I thought about my best friend, but who I thought about most…was her. I thought about all the things unsaid between people I love most and I, not the words themselves this time, but the idea of it…and something boiled in me, "How could this be happening?"

As the words shot holes in me, one after another, they made me think about her, about who I wanted to be for her and how I put a carefully chiseled statue in front of her time after time. The truth sprang up about many things, a truth I may not remember past this moment but it stood in front of me with monstrous ferocity - not as a god, not as a mountain, not as a grown-up as a child sees one…it stood smack in front of me, looking me dead in the eye, no taller than me, yet high above, scorning me for my neglect and also forgivingly understanding, making it that much greater than I. Then, I saw how beautiful it was. The ugly truth pushed and shoved at me with each period. I couldn't ignore it anymore and could hardly stand it altogether. That feeling of tears filled-up behind my eyes and subsided with the more and more quickly changing of the tide inside.

I could hardly believe how hard some of this was hitting me and the power of simplistic reality with which it spoke. It became awe-inspiring and rooted itself deep within my being, and I allowed it to, perhaps even encouraged it in my small fear. A sentence caught my attention more exactly. This was a very well-versed story. I became more and more impressed with its simple eloquence of view. I read along, hoping to find this piece as intriguing as I imagined it might be, though I was initially reading it because I had to.

When I started, I wasn't sure if this was the story or a review of it. It had a very peculiar opening (which was a good sign). I picked it up from a list of six stories, a couple of them sounded interesting, others as exciting as digging a hole just to fill it back in. I looked at the list of assigned readings and "Sonny's Blues" jumped out at me.

Ball and Chain
10072011

I remember one night
We had a big fight
I walked out and found a bench
Beneath a streetlight

She left the house
To try and get me back
I don't remember what we fought about, now
Looking back

As I sat on the bench
She curled up at my feet
Wrapped her arms around my leg
Drifted off to sleep
I stared down at her long
I looked at her hard
That soft face
The one burned in my head
Left a scar
I can't help but reminisce
On little moments like those
I convinced myself she wasn't
Just another one of those

I'm looking at life
Through the eyes of a smile
But pretending to be happy
Gets old after a while
When the time comes
To face the way I feel
I can't tell the difference from
What I should feel
And which feelings are real

I'm a fugitive now
My feelings joined the chase
Running away from my emotions
On a daily bas-is

Loss of Interest
10142011

Static Everything
10312011

What is progress?
One step in front of the other
Taking me nowhere
One hour after another
Doesn't get me there

Is it how close I am to where I'm going?
Is it how far I am away from what I'm trying to get away from?
Another to stack on the other
But I'm in the same place I was before
Another job
Another degree
Another girl
What's it matter to me?

What makes the difference between
Here and there?
Then and now?
I want to move
But don't know how
One decision to the next
Transition to the next context
Static everything

Affirmation
11102011

Will I fade into the back?
Where will I be when they're handing out medals?
Did I miss the train?
One great song about the angst of youth
One great painting immortalizing some truth
One great organization that saved the world
One great man who did it all

I am the one
So great and achiev-ed
I am the greatest man
Yet to be
I will accomplish
Everything

I want to be
The man of my dreams
Who took life by the horns
And did everything

The money
The clothes
Fuck all that
I'd be happier on a budget
I just want to live my dreams
I just want to be everything I know I can be
I just want to fulfill my expectations for me
From anybody and everybody including me
It's not too much to carry
I'm just feeling so small
Overwhelmed by the gravity of doing it all
Afraid to take a single step into a pitfall

One Great Day
I'm gonna be One Great Man
Who lived One Great Life
Which will be the tree so many hang their smiles on
That so much good has grown from
That has provided for those near and far in need
And the tree for the weary traveler to lean beneath for shade

The Sky is on Fire Tonight
11192011

The sky is on fire tonight
Clouds reflecting ambient light
Engines hum quiet
While cricket buzz riots
The sky is on fire tonight

Traffic lights blazing red
No one goes
Til the permission of green
Caravans of cops come and go as they please
Red and blue spreading a law-enforcing dis-ease
There is no one living in sight
The sky is on fire tonight

Orange of the streetlights
The slow of yellow
White from the stars
Through the clouds does not show
The sky is on fire tonight

Time-lapse turns streets into rivers of light
Burning a grid on the earth
As creatures of darkness play and matches alight
The city burns to the ground as I recline in delight
The sky is on fire tonight

Guilty Pleasures
11242011

Car beats poetry banging pavement
against my feet
Breeze sifting
Ease slowly into my seat
Holy day of thanks for this holiday

I blank

My words are failing for what I
have to say
Prayers to martyrs in remembrance
for things I never learned
Giving thanks for presence I never
earned
The ones who do are working
overtime

Stoking the fire
Hope is a fire
While the third world is burning
And choking
On fire

Not a care in the world outside of
my world
But everybody wants a piece of my
ass, fighting
Just enough money for that Xbox
360 Black Friday night
Village burning down somewhere
into the black of night
Oh, dammit! Somebody done stole
my new bike

I can't commune with God because
his profile is set to private
So, I'll hack it
Troll attack it
Then like it

My touch screen's only 1080p
Not HD enough for me to feel
purity
Surrounded by sounds in Dolby
Digital 5.1 mounding into a cloud
Surmount the cacophony by
slipping on Made in China
headphones on so I can slip away

Fall into the depths of forever alone
In my head

Give thanks for what I'm with while
others are without
THANK YOU, GOD, SO MUCH!
From my lungs, I shout

Can I enjoy the fruit of labor when
it's spoiled rotten by the suffering of
my neighbor?

The city I'm from is only street-
deep
It's all the same earth once you dig
underneath
How can I represent after all I've
refused to see?
How much more darkness behind
the smokescreen?

The necessities are bare minimum,
undressed
I may have more while others have
less
But I just want to give thanks, so I
digress

25

Insights
12312011

Enlightenment is the ability to cease thought.

Maturity is the ability to accept imperfection.

Ignorance is falsely believing (and more importantly, believing that others believe falsely).

This is what I realized based on what I've experienced and observed thus far.

Personal truth is the only truth.

The truth is always within reach and it is worth pursuing.

Perspective is not seeing something new the same way, it is seeing the same thing different ways, and requires creativity; this is why creativity is freedom.

Arguing beliefs is like arguing the colors of the rainbow. Either:
        a.) We all see the same color with different names, or
        b.) we all see different colors with the same name. Either way, no matter who wins, you haven't changed the way anyone sees that color, just what they call it.

Reflections on Volume II

"From Me to You" is stained with the fresh blood of working through my first heartbreak. It spans 19 to 20 years old, from 2010-2011. It felt as if that girl took my heart with her to sell out of that meat truck to anyone with enough tickets to buy it, eat it out of a wax-paper wrapper, and drop the remnants in the fairground mud. I opened up for the first time in my first serious relationship, and it ended in the Hindenburg.

I came to terms with the fact that my father was an ocean away, had my half-sister, and wanted to reconnect after I'd decided shut him out of my life for about eight months (regular reminders from my mother that, "you need to have a relationship with your father" may have helped persuade me). I replied to an email. I picked up the phone. I answered a video chat. I bought the ticket. I stayed with him in Greece for a full summer. We played a lot of catch-up. I met my sister: love at first sight. I didn't speak any Greek. She didn't speak any English. We gestured our way through connection.

So, I'm navigating the abandoned woods of (re)building a relationship with my father after more than eight years apart, grieving my broken heart, battling depression, meeting my eight-year-old sister and Greek family, all during my first time in abroad at the ripe age of 19. Fun, right? Kind of. Mostly confused and hopeless.

Side story: I found brief summer love with a girl named Konstantinas (Greek people are very…traditional with their names; she went by Nadia). Pretty sure she was cheating on her boyfriend, who was away on required military service, though this is uncorroborated. Beggars can't be choosers, and irony is bittersweet.

Anywho, I had a golden opportunity to experiment with independence in this foreign land, and I occasionally engaged. I could legally drink! I went to music festivals! But, again, for the most part, I just kept my nose in my journal, too sad to pursue any of the nine out of ten beautiful women walking around the most beautiful country on earth.

Upon returning stateside with the words of my father, "You're a man, now," branded on my heart, I found the band falling apart due to everyone getting a life. My mom convinced me to go on a college tour after months of pestering. I liked the campus and philosophy. They told me I didn't have the credentials to get in. I didn't like that, so I started community college to build my transcripts. I got a few jobs and learned how to bust my ass for my own sake. I got into the habit of going on categorically *long* night walks to decompress. I enjoyed the idea of being the last person on earth, the quiet, the cool air (a welcome break from the penetrating Florida sauna). I often fantasized about running into the one perfect girl who was walking around at night to clear her head like I was. One night, I found something else.

Florida is a…special place, filled with opportunity. For me, I was the opportunee and the Pinellas County Sheriff's Office was the opportuner. After several hours of night moseying, a friend and I were five minutes from our neighborhood. Details aside, I unknowingly cussed at a pair of police officers, and they responded in kind by shoving my face into the pavement at two in the morning with no witnesses. I learned what "no contest" means. I learned about overcrowded jails. I was released shortly after my arrival. Restrictions were imposed on my life. I lost my job for a "no call, no show."

I got a job at another restaurant, got involved in a class action lawsuit after quitting there, and started to contemplate what I wanted for my life. For instance, reapplying to the college that told me I couldn't get in, dabbling in photography, and picking up trombone (just in time to play for that ska band that didn't exist anymore).

> Reclaim your past
> It's who you are
> The familiarity of your former strangeness//

Volume /III//

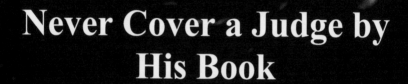

Never Cover a Judge by His Book

01052012 //
05192012

Age 20

Potential is the Currency of Fate
01052012

This is not
A new chapter of my story to be told
This is
A deepening of my heart-shaped hole
I threw caution to the wind
So I go wherever it blows
I made up my mind
But lost my marbles in the old
I see myself
And the shame that I feel
How could it be
I'm still stuck right here

Wherever I fall
I'm lying in wait
The truth is out there
My unarriven fate

I see the light at the end of the tunnel
It's a mirror at a dead end
If I break it
I'll be in the dark again

I look back at my progress
I peer ahead to my toll
It all looks the same
I'll sit here 'til I'm old

A life of simply doing what I'm told
A dream of one day breaking the mold

I invest in the losses
Look up to the demons
Recourse and repercussions
Won't bring me around

Am I really so lost?
Am I so hard to find?
Is anyone looking?
Is everyone blind?

The depth of the question
Ignorance of the answer
When it's all said and done
Comes the silent, grim necromancer

Young Demons
01232012

As if the words were a curse on me:

"I never knew you were so serious."

"You lack nothing."

Indignant I am to such praises and phrases
Though the definition of the word is lost amongst hazes
I never knew how much I had known, I had thought
My pleasantries stay only in phases

The sense that I make
Is the sense that I take
I sense that that sense
Is only a fake

Now I pass through the day as scrambled as eggs
The sunny-side-up turned over-hard in some way
Looking for answers to pleas of "Why me?"
I find an abundance and get lost in pity

My demons are new
They were just born today
Everything would get better
If they just go away

I scream and I yell
As I throw sticks and stones
So they're as hurt as I am
So they're just as alone

I'm afraid to make sense of
The sense I don't make
I'm afraid to admit
What I made was a mistake

I can never go back
I can never return
For better or worse
I can just watch it burn

Unrest
04122012

Getting miffed at all the opportunities I missed
All the times I thought I was giving so much
Looking back I see I could have given so much more
And of course, all the girls of my past
I cared so much about them and what we had
The feelings I felt all shattered like glass

Is my destiny lying broken on the floor?
I don't know but all my life I've been told
I'm capable of so much more
Faced with life decisions
I don't wanna get my hands dirty
Will I be stuck in indecision 'til I'm thirty?
When will I learn from the mistakes I made before?
When will I earn the will to wake up and soar?

I get so frustrated
Give-up
And I don't know why
To make it in the end I know I at least gotta try
Even as I'm sitting on this bench writing this song
I feel like what I'm doing is always wrong
Well, if I keep on sitting here, I'll never stand tall

I'm itching for success like bug bites in the Everglades
But I'm stressing over losing myself in the money I don't make
I already feel like I'm sacrificing relationships to a volcano
Sacrificing who I love so I can be the hero
Is concentrating on myself the vanity I run from?
Is staring in the mirror the only way to stardom?

Unsure what to do with the talent within me
Cocky as a motherfucker in what I could be
Will gloating of hypocriticals keep me tied to a tree?

Working five days bussing tables, the other two at school
Feel like I'm working my ass off but I'm just a fool
Not goal-oriented so I'm wasting my efforts and time
Everyone I know is going somewhere while I'm left behind

I'm just pissed-off every night before I go to sleep
Trying to build-up every day the pace I can keep
So exhausted by the end of the day
So burnt-out I can't even pick up the trombone I want to play

Even though I'm 20, still living at home
Saving my twenties in a jar to buy some transportation
There's so much in my head that I want to get done
Little things of this and that on the side just for fun

I got the bucket list posted-up on my textured white wall
Wish I could get up one day, rip it down, and do them all
But the reality of where I'm at is not where I'm gonna be
The question, "Where will I end up?" is burning in me constantly

I need to be the best I can cuz I carry my grandfather's name, Constantine
I can't allow the fear of failure to shy me away from my dreams
I can't think myself into a hole of negativity
I can't waste my time fearing all the negative possibilities
In the end, the only one to look out for me is me
But still, I'm helping-out everyone else leaving no time for me
Well, what about me, Constantine?

I'm supposed to be number one
Even if I live by the pen, then I'll die by the gun
When everybody else is walking is when I wanna run
When everybody else is talking is when I shut the fuck up
And I'm the one spitting compliments while the crowd is dissing
Cuz even if it kills me, I will be the exception to everyone
Against the grain, the one insane, I maintain my own
A wild child make you smile while I wind it up
Acting crazy, being lazy's gotta get up and go
I gotta give my all or fall from losing everything I have
Cuz dreams don't come true too easy
And I want mine so bad

There's nothing wrong with playing it smart
To be on the safe side
But if it's better safe than sorry
I'll be sorry I missed out

Samaine
05042012

Why God?
Must every man be pushed to his brink?
Why God?
Must every man sink?
Why God?
Must a man lose all he has to see what he had?
Are the lessons we've learned
Not the bridges we've burned?
Every time we turn our backs
We look back in regret

Why God, must we suffer?
To eat one another?
Why God, does such evil
Reside in the feeblest hearts of man?

It is all I can stand
I stand by with my own indignant hands

The Coming of...
05062012

Is a man made by the women he conquers?
Is a man made by the nights that he squanders?
Is a man made by the strength of his arm?
Is a man made by how much he can harm?
Is a man made by the size of his waist?
If these things are what make him
He's a man put to waste

A man is tempered by the heat he can stand
To stay cool under pressure in the face of demand
A man is undeterred by challenge or fire
Not quaking beneath the fulfillment or folly of desire
A man is not seen by the height of his tower
But the inch he gets up when beaten and battered
A man can be heard by his reason and laugh
Not the level of anger when he's yelling and crass
A man is not remembered by the length of his grudge
His forgiveness will lift him above any judge
A man is not recognized for the facade that he wears
Inside he is true, so the truth he must wear
A man is not felt by the back of his hand
An open palm, offering himself
Is the true sign of a man

Rejection
05192012

235 contacts in my phone
And somehow, I'm still left alone
Send a text to 15 people
And only get two back
You people don't even have the courtesy
To hit a friend back

Why do I even bother?
And why the fuck should I care?
It's not about ride or die
It's just being there

You fuckers can't acknowledge
That I even exist
Instead of a text message
Next time, I'll send you my fist

Ever since I can remember
It's been me, myself, and I
So alone in this world
But never a thought of suicide

Cast out and estranged
From the strangers around me
So many times I've hit the last straw
I smash my foot to the ground
Man, fuck 'em all

And don't think you're any different
If you're hearing this song
You're all the same bastards
With which I couldn't get along

Misunderstood by everyone
Including myself
So I guess I'll live my life
Alone, by myself

Reflections on Volume III

The third installment of my life on paper constitutes my striving for something more. In 2011 through 2012, I was still 20 years old. You see, the thing is, I tend to write most when I need to process my more challenging emotions, so the content of "Never Cover a Judge by His Book"—really every volume—is crusted over with the scabs of loneliness and rejection. I wasn't ready to let go of my pain. So much happened in such a short amount of time, I believe I couldn't properly focus on healing any one wound, such that they became a bucket of discarded acrylic paint, individual colors poorly mixed into that disappointing brown. Overall, this volume represents the final throes of throwing off the "ball and chain" of that dumb, beautiful, adolescent sorrow.

Outside of my writing, I actually had a lot of things going well for me. Believe it or not, I actually started to believe in myself again…unbelievable. This happened in the most literal sense. I got a tattoo of Cassiopeia on my calf, because it almost exactly resembled a symbol my night-walking buddy and I had made as something of a joke for "Constantism," a mock philosophical religion I'd created back in middle school out of satire and distaste for the franchised dogma of big religion when I was exploring my spirituality. When I learned about the constellation in astronomy class—a personal favorite college course—I was floored when I realized the resemblance to the symbol we'd made in MS Paint, and I took it as a sign to be and believe in who I am, so I put it on my body.

I almost got straight A's for the first time in my life (my one B out of five possible A's was three percent shy due to skipping a quiz to see the Red Hot Chili Peppers). I met one of my idols at the time, Saul Williams, after dancing my face off at his show, and I got a moment to show him my journals (I blame him for planting the seed: "You need to publish these"). I joined honor societies. I bought a scooter (RIP Desmond: jet-black and chrome, 49cc Vespa-esque stallion, whose motor baffled mechanics by its sudden dysfunction). I began experimenting with doing more things solo and sober, and building a better relationship with myself, which, at the time, just felt sad and pathetic—to be "taking myself out." However, I did acknowledge on some level that I was consciously trying to move past the wall of apathy which was holding me back, and that held some reward. I started taking ownership for my life and the power I have to choose. I shifted from focusing on myself because I was sad to focusing on myself because I wanted more.

The past is dead
But the dead are not forgotten//

Volume //IV//

The Sounds, Something to Die For

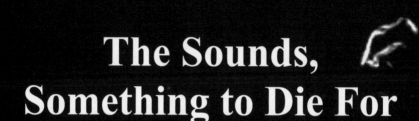

09092012 // 12112013

Ages 21- 22

Call and Resolve
09092012

Where truth is a realm
Reached not by fact
But through Power of Expression

Breaking the threshold of
Withheld wit
Withering whines
And worrisome pines for

Prostration
Pontification
Enunciation
To reconcile and shun
The suffix "-tion"

For it's worn from overuse
Loosely defined
Out of my mind

Metaphors may lack fours
But every once so often
An F's gotta lay back
To make me phat
To make an impact

To my peers and perceivers
See-ers and believers
I hyphenate you
My friends

Just on the end
Because in The Beginning
Black became Light
A bold black scratch from the match strike
Separating vows from vow-els

In this realm
A Belief Can Dance
Exaggerating Feels Grotesque
H I J K L M N O Prose

Spelling bees
Buzz through the air
Making honey for our ears
And off in the distance
Not too far away
Words of inconsequence
Just something to _____

The River, Water, and Flow
09152012

The toxins in the water beneath your feet
Soak up into your skin
Inside
Compiles
A build-up that's breaking you down

The blood, sweat, and tears in the river you're in
Are chemical compounds
Cleanse yourself
In the dirt of everyone else

Once you're infected
You perpetuate the river of Hell, well
Breathing in
Is only half of what's required
To cope with the fire of Hell
Breathing in
What you're taking in is the pain, disdain of it all
Breathing in
Even the river evaporates, precipitates in the clouds
Breathing in

And out
Let the rain come down
The cycle repeating
But at least you're breathing
Don't forget to
Let it out

Surface Tension
09182012

I don't know how much longer I
can keep this up
I don't know how much longer I
can keep this up
I can't keep this up
I can't keep this up
I can't keep this up
Up up up up

Before I get stuck
Before I get fucked
When I run out of luck
By that time I'll be
Hooked

Fish on a line
Strung-out
Send my love on a wire
Hanging by a thread

Pull me out of the water
I'll hang 'til I'm
Dead

Pretending to be
Me for a day
But what can I say?
Everyone else has already said it all

So what can I do but fall
In line
That same line that holds my head
above water
Keeps me breathing the oxygen
Absent of hydrogen

Parched is my soul
The dry air takes its toll
I'm a fish out of its bowl
I have no control

Underwater, the sound is dampened
Purified through surface tension
Laughter in ridicule
The downtrodding habitual

I can't make-out too clear, but I
know it's there

But I'm free to ignore and swim in
my own sea
To see what I can see in my own
sea
Inside of me

The comments are murmurs and
buzzing above
Looking down they chit-chatter as
I'm searching for _____
Fishing for fish, I'm a fish that's
fishy
And that's it
And there's no longer anything
special about it

I don't know how much longer I
can keep this up
I don't know how much longer I
can keep this up
I can't keep this up
I can't keep this up
I can't keep this up
Up up up up

Unlearning and forgetting
Everyone that I've done
How do I get back to where I've
begun?

Square one is fictitious
A vicious nightmare presented as a
dream
Neither is real
Both less than they seem
Lines are drawn in my head and
they're crossed every time
Build me up
Break me down
Mess me around
Do you know what I've found?

I'm no better than the day I started
Is that the nature of things?
Or am I just broken-hearted?

And if I haven't made any headway
since that first fateful day

Am I back at square one?
Or lost in decay?

A stand-alone complex is simple as
they come
Either find someone to grow old
with
Or end-up alone
Yea, one may walk through The
Valley of the Shadow of Death
Unafraid
But alone, he will crumble
For it's pointless to stay

A wise man once said
"There's only one way out"
But I was told that is wrong
So I'm stuck sticking around

I'm forced to look around and find
something to see
By default, life is beautiful
If it wasn't, we'd be
Drowning
Wallowing
In this miserable sea

The ocean is vast
And the horizon never ends
We're told over and over
And over again
The possibilities are endless
Look to what lies ahead

Nowhere to run
Nowhere to hide
No one to turn to
No reason to lie

What's on my mind?
I'll give you a piece
But take one little bite
And you've caught my disease

I won't beg you to listen
Won't ask you to stay
The last time I tried that
I found myself astray

"Misery loves company"
At least, that's what they say
So make yourself comfortable
We're in this together
Either way

Paper Towels
09302012

Wincing away at the once-bright star that is my hopes and dreams
I pass by the people trading complaints on the streets

Time ticks by one dish at a time
Blisters and cuts and scrapes
Soak in dishwater leftovers
Working my hands to the bone
Whole molecules slip past one another
It's raining sand

I'm moving up in the world
I got arrested today
One little F-bomb in the wrong direction
And the cops had to teach me a lesson
I can't do shit until I'm off probation

There's no hope in sight
So I'm riding into the rain
What am I
But one man against the rest

Out of Context
09302012

Everything is simply
Taken out of context

An object misplaced
Roles erased

Everything is simply
Taken out of context

Non-objective beauty
Abstract disunity

Everything is simply
Taken out of context

Quarter-note, half-rest
Syncopated silence stressed

Everything is simply
Taken out of context

Me beside the ocean
Drowned in a sound

Everything is simply
Taken out of context

Seek insight outside the lines
Basic structure compromised

A grand prize of grandeur in reprise
Cast a stone into the pond
A wave arises with help from the wind

Everything is simply
Taken out of context

Sought in thought
Fought with situation

Context is simply
Everything taken out

Hex
11272012

Faced in battle
Lay a finger on my hair
If you dare
But beware
I shall not spare you
Cast my demons to despair you
Whatsoever misfortune befalls you

Here on out
Without a doubt
I'm the cause affecting your resolve
Scarred by my cursed tiger's claw
I promise you shall rue the day
You stepped and threatened to betray

Today will not be the last you see of me
Your nightmares shall be ruled by me
Your dreams will be consumed
And every waking second you take pause to catch your breath

I will crawl out from behind your head
To whisper in your ear
Just so you can hear

All your dreams and insecurities
Demons and self-doubt
Every worry, ache, and pain
Your heart has known since your first air

And when you crumble from the horror
Crying out, "It's not fair!"
Remember
It was on this day
I told you to beware

Observer Noir
12152012

Do you know the silence of the night?
You can hear the rubber soles of your shoes
Gripping and leaving the concrete beneath you
You can hear a car coming, five miles away

Do you know the darkness of the night?
Shadows cast in front of you from dull light sources
Every street and traffic light
Accompanied by the occasional pair of headlights

Do you know the reflection of the night?
You can hear your skin stretch
When you look too far to look over your shoulder
Every sinew groans in your eardrum
Cartilage creaks between your bones
The rush of air through your nostrils
Howls through your windpipe
And bellows through the expanding tissue of your lungs
Suddenly, you're aware your ribcage has joints too

Do you know the silence of the night?
Your heartbeat surfaces as audible as
A leaf crashing to earth a half-block away
Under the roar of blood rushing through your veins
Every moment of every second you've ever been alive
You begin to feel, coursing under your skin

Have you heard silence?

Have you seen darkness?

Have you been sleeping?

You know not what surrounds you

Have you not heard the whispers behind the external hum of your thoughts?
It calls from underneath
As you sleep through habitual ignorance
A train wreck occurs at a frequency
Below the threshold of the human ear

Do you know the darkness of the night?
Because it knows you.

BOOM!
12152012

My ambitions blow my dreams to smithereens
Never becoming fully realized
And thus
Never concrete

My wishes smash the dishes which serve the desserts of my desires
And on the side, my deep-fried fantasies
Are thrown out of the frying pan and into the fire

My hope burns to a butt
Like a joint full of dope
Through my telescope, I look to the horizon
Fantasizing about

One day

But Oneday is not a day of the week
So I'm stuck on an island
All my dreams were just islands in the sky
Lost in the clouds

I never learned how to fly
The fleeting beating of time
Progresses by the pulsation of imagination

My goals were sucked into black holes just as they became
Matter of fact

When I was a child
My thoughts ran wild
But after a while
My youth fell away
Into decay
Tomorrow is hollow
Echoing yesterday's dreams

The World Is Our Playground
12222012

No one can see the end result
No one knows where this is going
The king could end up a peasant
A peasant, the king
All I have is this journal to keep me company on this Saturday night

I do not reach out to the world
Instead
I wait for the night to grab me and drag me from my confines
Locked from inside
You'll have to knock first for my approval
If your games do not meet my amusement
I will tear away and wonder what might have come, had I come

The world is a place to envy through the looking glass
Envy and curiosity splinter me from the inside-out
I prick my heart on my own hardened edges
A cold wind slices through the slivers and gaps

The warmth of yesterday's sun flees the cold rising of the moon
The height of night brings relief
At last, all remaining energy of the day dissipates
And I venture out into the deserted streets

Everything is still

All is lost and there are no more complications

This is
Absolute freedom
Alone

I uncover moments of satisfaction buried by the day
The silence
It slowly carves a bleeding smile into my cheeks
I close my eyes and fill every crevice with crisp air
Untainted by other mouths
Through my cracks
I become cool

Carbon Paper
12302012

Do you think the human race will be around a billion years from now?
In a 13.7 billion-year-old expanse of universe, we are
The beginning of a spark
In a 20 billion-year-old universe
That's all we ever will be

However
That beginning of a spark will forever be a phenomenal story of
Art
Beauty
Emotions
And development

It's the little things in life
And in the life of the universe
We are one of the littlest–and certainly–most beautiful things to ever occur
If we are, indeed, a spark of life
Then we need fuel to burn

The more we burn
The brighter we shine
The earth is dying because of us
So be it

We are not long for this existence
Prolonging it will only bear witness to our slow decay
Glazing over our glory

Home Doesn't Feel the Same Anymore
01152013

Right now...
At this very moment...
I am sitting in the room of my childhood on the hand-me-down bed of
my mother, covered by the comforter stained with memories back to when my
years filled one hand. On the floor to my left is a pile of patchwork which has
endured my adolescence as my backpack. To my right, a TV tray supporting a
bowl of Frosted Flakes (a childhood delicacy), an iPad Mini from Christmas, on
top of which is a hand-me-down cell phone, the service for which is paid for by
my mother. Beyond the nostalgic TV tray, itself; a dresser marked and spray
painted with the inner conflict and fear which begets a boy faced with becoming a
man.
Over my left shoulder, I glance a sticker-strewn door, the gatekeeper of
my privacy, seal of the bubble of ignorance containing a world where I never
need grow up, under my mother's roof, which I do not pay for, nor do I make a
particular point to see that the house is as clean and well-kept as the best of my
ability and free time would allow. I am surrounded by things, I see my reflection
in their every surface and within them; however, I do not see any muscle tone nor
facial hair. They echo a voice still taught with youth. I am surrounded by things,
yet each morning and each night these things become less present in my heart.
A decade and more in this cube. Its walls lined with my musk. Its carpet
spotted with a memoir of constellations in food and drink and age, creating a
story of hideous mosaic. Dingy. Tired. These walls, this ceiling, and carpet have
seen more than my days here, and they are almost as weary of me as I am of
them. All of these things are mine, but very few of them belong to me.
With each day that passes I grow more insane over my lack of growth. I
feel stifled by the memories calling to me from each item like an old companion
whom one must say goodbye to and move on but dreads the guilt and remorse of
doing so. I am pacing at the crossroads. The higher path has offered me my higher
education at the cost of my independence. Below, I see myself in a life I am
solely responsible for. Between is a wood too thick to penetrate by any means
save the imagination - this is the best of both worlds, an impossibility. Up ahead I
cannot see beyond the hills of the unknown. I merely fancy what I am told lies
beyond by those who have long-crossed the valleys. These paths are my own, and
I may take either at any time. For now, I take solace in my responsibility for that
choice. For now, I wait.
23:29 PM

Playing Tetris with my Life
022242013

       Threw away more stuff, put the dresser in my closet, made a donation pile for tomorrow. My room will be reduced to two stacked mattresses, a TV tray, two small shelves of DVDs and books, a bass guitar, trombone, hand drum, a grill from the front-end of a school bus, and a handful of variously sized paintings. Everything is else carefully tessellated into my closet in 3 milk crates, 5 boxes, a suitcase, a small pile of toolboxes, and a lawn chair.

Charlotte
04202013

What does a spider think about
As it hangs there lying in wait?
Does it contemplate its next meal
Ensnared in its silky strait?
Does it think of past meals it's eaten?
Or the beasts it one day will eat?
Does it pick through its favorites?
Or salivate at the thought
Of a fly that is warm and sunbaked?

Does a spider have hopes?
Or dreams?
Or aspirations?
In which it confides and remakes?

Does a spider form concepts?
Or base understandings?
Of how identities are
Se - par - ate?

When a spider beholds the world
Through its eight tiny eyes
Does its mind's ninth eye reflect and relate?

What is a spider's view of the world?
And commentary on how it operates?
Does a spider engage in self-chatter?
Does it remonstrate, reprise and resink?

As it tends to the task of mindless repetition
In buildings its rambler's keep
Does a spider daydream?
Does a spider imagine?
Does a spider have a full range of human emotions?

Does a spider wonder if it could do better?
What about how much it's accomplished?

Does a spider feel pressure from its spider society?
Experience guilt?
Or jealousy?
Or affection?

Does a spider enjoy spinning its web?
Does its life have direction?

Condensation
04232013

Life breathes glimpses of hope
Love breeds warmth in the night
The sun peeks over the horizon twice
The moon bleeds its light for the lost
Air dances together in thick fog
Dreams sweat over puddles of ink

Afraid to Fall
08282013

In this hour of 10:00 in the evening
On this day of Wednesday, August
28th
In this year of two-thousand and
thirteen
At this age of twenty-two
At this New College of Florida

I find myself
Unhappy
I apply this to
A direction
I feel I am moving in an unhappy
direction
Internally

Looking back
Looking forward

Pressure
Responsibility
Discomfort
Transition
(Non) Dedication to decision
Renewal
Purgatory
Limbo
Drifting
Low

These are all words I attach to
Hold on to
Latch on to
My "situation"
Why these quotations?
Am I not giving credit where credit
is due?
Am I undermining the gravity?
The difficulty
Intensity
Of what is
Has been
And is to come?

Certainly, I am not the only one
Surely, I am not the sun
Everything revolving around me
When I collapse

Gobbling-up and pulling down
You
And you
And you
I cannot be at the center of it all
I am not the only one afraid to fall

Ripples of Eternity
09232013

To watch the rain
Is to observe the nature of existence
Each raindrop a universe
An existence unto itself

God is in the clouds
A countless reign of Big Bangs
Into kaleidoscopic collapse
Rippling into one another
All collecting
Connecting in puddles
Originating from

God
Is in the clouds
Hypnotized as I am by the droplets
Softly fading into a puddle of
existence
This is resonating with my make-up

What makes-up me
A drop in the sea
In a drop in the sea
In a drop in the sea
In a drop in the sea
Within a drop
Explodes into a puddle
Waves of energy
Of matter
Of which I am
Insignificant
Or in signifying that I can't fathom
Just how many leagues I am
Under the sea I am
Under the sea I am
Under the sea I am

Layers upon layers
Smaller and smaller
Bigger and bigger
How little or how few
How many or how much more

A raindrop on the ground
Alone
There is no sound
But so many muster thunder

Where on the ground
We all the many burst and plunder
Ever-expanding at an accelerating
rate

Anticipate the very moment our
raindrop fades into the sheet of
calm
Dissolve into the puddle
Gone

Moment by moment
Person by person
Generation by era by eon by terra
by cosmos by universe by
multiverse by infinity by eternity
All dissolving
All absolving
All collecting in the calming,
quieting, subsiding, satiate,
flattened and stilled natural state

Take a breath to respirate

We have forever now
Until the next raindrop
Crash
De-still another forever yet
Until the last splash
The storm has reached its end
The sun comes out to play
And then
Dries up all the rain again
Forever now not far away
Rain come again another day

Blank Page
10152013

A new page
Another page
A different page
Yet remarkably the same as the
others

Full of potential because it is blank
It is mine to create
Each day I step out of the shower
Naked
Blank
Free to create me as I see fit

Who is this person I decide to be
every day?
What rules and restrictions have I
set for myself?
Well, isn't that what I'm here for?
To figure out who I am?
I'm not so sure that's the point

Some scars and tattoos have left
marks
Stories
Possible restrictions, but trivial
Every new day I decide to be
Me

Whoever that is
Whomever that may be
I have carefully constructed
Crafted
Formulated
My Self

Such a fleeting thing I am
This Me
Moments of pure insanity
Of surreality
Of the realization that I could do
anything completely unpredictable
Completely un-Me at any moment

Anyone could
Moments of deciding not to
Of eliminating the seemingly
outrageous

And living them to the bare
minimum
Disconsidering the alternatives
Taking these things, we would not
or could not or should not do
For granted

These things
These horrible things
Sometimes wonderful dreams
Nightmares
Endless possibilities of actions and
non-actions
Causes and effects
Items of insanity shelved on social
norms built by society
Us
We
I

Who am "I"?
What is "Me"?
What manner of creation am I?
Do I construct myself or do we?

Who came first in my perception?
The squawking chicken of society?
Or the unborn egg of me?
Who might I be?
At another place?
In another time?

It would seem that I am infinitely
malleable
Infinitely foldable and adaptable
It is simply different choices being
made
Small ones
Within the parameters which allow
my Self to remain

Difficulty due to indecision
Tangents
Possibilities
Regularities
Singularities
Alone

Alone
Free to create my Self
To be born or created as the first or
only person
It is up to me to decide
Completely free

Alone
I decide what my hands are for
Language
Thoughts before language are
abstract representations
Alone

What is a human?
Up to me
What is a person?
Up to me
Who am I?
Who is this Me?
Up to me
Completely free
No society
No squawking chicken
Just the egg

Close your eyes now
Silent…There is nothing…
Only the egg
Full of potential

I define myself by my surroundings
Strip away all I know to nothing
And I am nothing
In the blankness, there is me

No society
Interaction is slavery
Life is conformity with each added
element
Go back now

Blank
Just Me
Add a tree
With this one element, I am forced
to interact

This element will soon define Me
This one element beside myself

I will spend my life interacting with
that tree
Constructing Me, all along

I will climb it, stare at it
Trying to figure out its meaning
My meaning
Life's meaning
100 years of me, a tree, and nothing

Then it's over
That is existence for me
Infinite moments and endless
possibilities reduced to a simplified
attempted constant of a Self
Am I an extension of the tree or the
tree of me?

I could be reduced
But there's more
This vacuum
This void
This construct of regulations based
on decisions I never had the chance
to make for myself
Only choosing what was offered to
me

You see now
Look at me
See what I am, as far as you're
concerned, and what you make me
And so you are what I make you
The empty mind is full of
possibilities
But it is a slave to what it already
knows

So here I am
Here you are
Here we are
Welcome to my, your, our crisis
The existential crisis
The emptying
Deconstructing

It's complicated in the simplest way
or simple in the most complicated
way
I don't know for sure, but I'm here
to say that I have a problem

I think we all do
It is our turn to decide
The more we realize that
The more powerful we become

I am free to take the wheel, though
it is not my decision alone
Nor is it yours
Together, we decide

Voodoo Potluck
10312013

Slither and sizzle
Sizzling gristle
The roast is rotating over heat
The fire is simmered down into smoke
And slowly billows and blows
Entrails entangle the tastes of a mangled carcass
Skewered on a pole

Oh, though death's throes have clutched this poor pig's throat
The taste buds of the looming, consuming collective
Drown in saliva for sow
Blood drips from the lips of the damned
Both sacrificial rotisseries rotating

Seething with devious delight by the light of the fire
Demon bystanders are evenly drawn and repelled
By the smells and lashings of light
At last, they dive in and like vultures
And begin to ingest the innards
In grotesque unceremony

I Am _____
11222013

Every day will not be a triumph
Not every night a conquest
There is no prize nor contest
No promise for better, however

Whenever skies are grey
The light will cast a silver lining
Whenever sepia filter
Becomes not just an objective artistic expression
But a perception which dulls every vibrancy and excitement
Somewhere I can still find gold
Or at the very least, bronze

But to hang these precious medals around my neck
I have to earn them
Even though I already deserve them

Because the unfair fact of life is
The world is my oyster
But I must work
And learn
And earn
And toil away
Every single day
To find my pearl

But I have hope
I am hopeful
I am capable
I am strong
And though I have been wrong (from time to time)
I know my rights
And I will fight for them

And I have hope
I am hopeful
I am capable
I am inspired
I am _____

30 Essays in 30 Days
12112013

Dec. 11 - Alter Egos: Creating Them in the Modern Day: Facebook, Gamer Tags, Reality
Dec. 12 - Compare 2 Types of Poetry
Dec. 13 - Different Writing Processes
Dec. 14 - Blackhole & Multiverse Theory (3 Sources)
Dec. 15 - Influence of "Autobiography of a Yogi" on My Life
Dec. 16 - Tattoos I Have; why, where, when, what
Dec. 17 - History of My Backpack
Dec. 18 - A Day in The Life of Jackson Hughes
Dec. 19 - What Has Caused My Inflated Sense of Purpose
Dec. 20 - Why Did I Pick Psychology as My Career?
Dec. 21 - How to Make A Dog Listen (2 Sources)
Dec. 22 - The Evolution of The Plastic Revolution (3 Resources)
Dec. 23 - Some People Just Aren't Meant to Do Drugs (2 Sources)
Dec. 24 - Compare/Contrast Daoism/Shinto (3 Sources)
Dec. 25 - How to Deal with Stress (4 Sources)
Dec. 26 - Music: The Great Equalizer
Dec. 27 - 1 Great Product Idea & The Impact It Would Have
Dec. 28 - Proof of the Collective Consciousness (3 Sources)
Dec. 29 - My Learning Style and How to Use It (1 Source)
Dec. 30 - Tim Burton; Life, Careers, Art Commentary, Personality
Dec. 31 - My Application for the Mission to Mars (2 Sources)
Jan. 1 - Interpretations of the (Om, Ahm, Aum) (3 Sources)
Jan. 2 - Effective Study Methods (3 Sources)
Jan. 3 - What Country Will I Visit Next and Why? (2 Sources)
Jan. 4 - Compare/Contrast the 3 Learning Styles for ISP
Jan. 5 - How to Decide What to Do with Your Life
Jan. 6 - Why Value 'The Herd'? (Borges Argument)
Jan. 7 - Trombone in a Brass Gang Terrorizing the Woodwinds
Jan. 8 - Fictional Story; A Colony Who Lives in Treehouses (make it gory and violent)
Jan. 9 - Non-Fiction Story; Life of a Water Molecule (3 Sources)
Jan. 10 - A Piece of New College History (3 Sources)
Jan. 11 - The Fungus Among Us (3 Sources)

Reflections on Volume IV

A break in the status quo. "The Sounds, Something to Die For" starts at a crossroads in 2012, at 21 years old, between my old habits, old feelings, old ways of being, old perspectives, old pain, and the new. I had a decision to make. More girls were coming in and out of my life, but I remained distant. A mix of new accomplishments, old coping mechanisms, new challenges, and old stagnancy resulted in a deeper desire for change both inside and outside of myself.

My mom got cancer. I got accepted into New College. I started dreaming big and setting bigger goals for myself further down the line. My close friend group remained mostly the same, but the depth of relationships shifted. I started to develop brotherhood, and we planned trips of our own together. We started making pacts with each other.

I celebrated graduating with my Associate in Arts degree at St. Petersburg College by flying off to study Spanish in Spain on scholarship, after which I traveled solo on my own time and dollar through Italy and Greece (yes, of course I visited my dad and sister). I started feeling excited about life again. I flew home and immediately moved my entire life out of my childhood bedroom and into a dorm at New College.

Although I had a strong foundation of world perspective from my shaman mother, punk/ska influence, and travels abroad, I was not prepared for the challenges and education that would come from the liberal arts community. School-wide passive-aggressive attacks online against "less-woke" individuals were the norm. I love and support y'all, but *damn*...you have *got* to work on how you get your message across.

New College pushed my limits in many ways. A litany of essays in every class, each one longer on its own than most of my previous essays from community college combined. I nearly threw in the towel in my first semester because of my first double-digit-page essay (which ended-up being almost 20 pages after a pep talk from my professor). While I was enamored with college life and proud that I'd worked hard to get there, I didn't quite fit in because I was a transfer student, thus stepping into a pool of limbo with about 20 or so other misfits that had neither started the journey of New College with the rest of the students our age who'd already bonded deeply in their time together, nor completely fit in with the newest first-year students because they were just beginning their studies. I leaned towards the fresh blood, which was more inviting than the exclusive and established senior cliques within the microcosm of a student population smaller than my graduating class in high school.

The greatest gift and lesson from this period is that we all have a voice running in our heads all the time, and we can take an active role in that conversation. I learned that I can actively work on loving myself, and so I did. Now, if only I had somebody else to love me while I was loving myself...hmm.

> At first the cricket drove me nuts
> Chirping at all hours of the night
> Then, I started to acknowledge and accept it
> Now, it is my unseen lover//

Volume

//V///

What are You Doing for Others?

12222013 //
07072014

Age 22

Truth & Lie
12222013

Which creates the dividing line
The truth or the lie?
What is a lie?
Is it simply to omit the truth?
To obscure the truth?
To cover, to twist, or tell the complete opposite of the truth?
What definition exists for a lie without truth to oppose?

What is truth then?
To be true to something, oneself, a society, a promise, to fight for what is right?
No
These are all acts of truth

What is its essence?
Its state of being?
Is it the absolute? Absolution?
Is it the embodiment of commitment or consistency?
Can it simply be written-off as fact or common knowledge?
Verified or veritable?

What is a lie?
What makes a liar or an honest man?
No doubt it is in their actions
Should the truth be absolution?
A final act of decency or commitment or consistency resolves a man and reduces
him to either
A liar
Or honest
True to something
True to his word, whatever that word may be, blessed or damned

Is truth reducible to a single component or is it a sum of its parts?
Telling facts, consistency, committing, standing-up

Do not deny thy self
Know thy self
Lies, deceit, opportunism, silent obedience or consent in dishonest climate
Is the line black and white?
Does it vary by the situation?
Can it be case-by-case, or ultimate, or both?
Is it a lie to operate or assess case-by-case?
Honest to decide in ultimatums?

Discantled
01152014

Confined betwixt corner
A ruse or aroused?
Each slink
Ex - cit - ting

Such onslaught of senses
Every toe tip teeters
On the edge of the earth
Sounds smash into processes of
Smell, taste, touch, and sight

Fight and battle each titan
Crash
Thwack
Shink
Fwop

Lamp becomes lightning
Striking into sight
Unannounced tantalization
Air wafts palpable peril
ZZZZZZZZZAAAAAACCCKK
KKTTTSSSSHHHH!
A mosquito lands, aloof

Another ligament stretches
A tendon tenses
Muscle mounds
Thread spans the echoless chasm
To traverse a small room

Leaving the moment
Circumnavigating the universe
Returning to the next
Struggling to comprehend each
instant
From distance unfathomable

Even fear is a notion too clear to
grasp
Overwhelming is understate the
absence of understanding
Thoughts are not beyond
comprehension
Rather
Confounded by suggestion

Behind each sensation is the
momentum of the cosmos
Time is no less linear
But experienced instantaneously,
instead of successively

Insanity assimilates incessantly in
instances without warning
Bordering on the brink of
unbridled, bridgeless abysses
This is it
Always. Swaying. World. Under.
Tread.
Anticipation is the antithesis to
existence

Eggshells litter all paths ahead and
behead and behoof
These enormous pupils inside these
insignificant eyes
Fall short of encompassing all
incoming information forthwith and
hitherto

The calm before the storm is but the
blink of an eye
The see-faring sailor must brave a
new typhoon between blinks
Monsoons, mountains, hurricanes,
hills washout and overshadow
meager mites on a mouse

Trounce
In an instinct-tethered inkling
Doubt holds hands with action in
information in front of paralysis
Such is the life of the overwhelmed
cat

Plans & Traps
01222014

      This week has had many instances of my need to help. I often invite myself into others' problems. This isn't anything new, just forgotten. A recent trip through the journals jarred my memory and I was reminded of my knight-in-shining-armor complex. Always there to help. Maybe not so drastic as I make it out to be, but always more than happy to help. It brings me great satisfaction, makes me feel good.

      Psychology. Dr. Dhonau? A complex is binding. To face is it is to realize you're trapped. To accept it is to hold the key. When I hold my key, do I walk out into the unknown, or do I stick to the familiar? There is more than one career path out there for me. To believe otherwise is foolish, but as I lay here over my five journals, I'm trying to make sense of where my life is going, trying to decide where I think it should go. Do what makes you feel good. The only final decision is your own and you can change your mind at any time. For now, psychology is a good way to make a living guiding others and that's good enough. Too much time thinking to myself. Time to go outside and play some drums.

      12:07 PM

Where Will You Be in 10 Years?
01232014

      In 10 years, it will be January 23, 2024. I will be 32 years old. I will be done with all my schooling. I would like to be living in the mountains, preferably in Latin America. I will be playing another instrument or two on top of having mastered hand drum, trombone, and harmonica. My job will be very much hands-on. Some of my work will be with children as a mentor, other parts involve building and working with plants. I want a good woman with me that complements me. She doesn't have to be the last woman in my life, but an important one, one that makes me lemon ginger tea and other comfortable things when I'm having a hard time. I want clean air, a long day of activity that I can smile about, and a hard night's sleep. Sugar gliders, hedgehogs, dogs, chameleons…I'd like a few pets in my family.

A Version of Characterization
01222014

Is this the place for me? Is this the path I wish to take? Big picture, guy. Big picture. Management, supervisor. Comes-off as an asshole. Overwhelmed by small tasks and can't handle them, better suited to directing on a larger scale. Guidance. Mentor. Good at teaching. One thing at a time, one step at a time. Very meticulous, very calculating, very organized. Bites-off more than he can chew on a regular basis. Bitches about it. Keeps doing it to challenge himself. Likes, no, loves to challenge himself, push his boundaries. When he doesn't want to do something, he doesn't do it, plain and simple. However, he hates failure. He hates admitting defeat. He hates vulnerability and weakness. He hates the notion of being less-than. Highly competitive in a very covert way. There are times when he challenges himself and gets into situations where he does not like what he's doing and has every resistance to doing it, but his drive to succeed, to not admit defeat (to himself or anyone else), it backs him into a corner within himself. He is torn between his ideals of doing only what he declares worthy of his energy and preventing himself from failing. 9 times out of 10 he pushes through because his drive to succeed is greater. He will talk himself into it, convince himself that - in the bigger picture - this is a step that must be taken to do what he wants to do in the future. It is a small loss of interest for a greater victory of dreams.

Full of ideas and dreams and advice for others. Loves collaboration, teams, accomplishing things together and bonding through that process, the process of problem-solving. Loves solving problems. Can't get enough. Everything is a problem and once it's solved: great satisfaction. One problem to the next, whether it's his own or someone else's. The greatest problem he could face is when there is no problem to solve, no dilemma, or crisis. Solving a problem right now while writing this. Ever-investigating himself. Getting to the never-attainable core: his essence. Wants to know what makes him tick. Extremely satisfied with the progression of this paragraph, as a matter of fact. Loves to know what makes others tick. Pushes people's buttons to see what makes them happy and what bothers them. Loves to watch, analyze, engage as minimally and effectively and efficiently as possible to obtain information. Problems to solve everywhere.

People are the ultimate riddle? Psychology. That is why. "Eureka!" so to speak. (quotations, writing quotations in parentheses, so to speak in quotations). It's outrageous. Loves wordplay and poetry and puns because it's all more problems. A journal starts with a problem. These things are outside of myself and I have to figure things out for myself. Tick. Tick. Tick. Tick. Self-exploration.

The Hardest Days Are the Ones When You Are Hardest on Yourself (Dear C)
01302014

      Listen man, the things you set out to do, you do them. It may not be as perfect as you expect yourself to believe and perform, but you accomplish your goals, best means necessary. You do things on your own terms and the only person you ever compromise with is yourself. You're always the last one you can convince. Trust yourself, even forget yourself every so often. It's okay! Too tough, tough guy. Well, I guess it's gotten you this far, right? I just wonder if things couldn't have been a little easier along the way, a little more enjoyable; if they couldn't be that way now. Sure…you can go on this way. You'll make it through and get the things you want, but you may never be alright. Chill. Lower the bar, at least low enough that you can clear it to get over the wall, if not someone else, a woman. Life does not have to be challenge after challenge, inside and out. Soften up. Let love in. You have made some small steps and they've been helpful. The real challenge, for you, is to take that leap, to drop your guard and just be alright. But there is no rush. There is no pressure. There is no way better than the way you feel is best.

      Best,
      C.

      00:27 AM

Regret
02022014

Gunshot waves scream across the beach
For an instant
Then
Cease
Sway
Sizzle
And retreat
Leaving me be
An eternity
Passes between
Each
Moment I live for
The shore recoils
In serenity

Dear Dad
02042014

I don't anticipate this ending in tears, but who knows, could dig some things up. I just thought it would be nice to write something to you, even if only symbolically.

It seems like I'm writing a letter to a dead person, or at least someone inaccessible, based on those few lines. You're only an email away, Skype call every now and again, could even be just a phone call if I put the effort in to figure it out. Even still, you feel so far away from me, or I feel so far away from you. It looks as though I'm avoiding you, that I can't be bothered or I'm afraid. Could it be spite? The whole idea of writing this, saying and asking these things to myself seems stupid, but I'm doing it anyway.

Well, as far away as you may be and lacking as our communication is, you're still with me day to day: this half of the dorm is disgustingly organized. Moving to this new place really has given me new opportunities to grow and allow myself to evolve. The times I go home I can see my habits revert back to what they were. I think it will always be that way; associating things like that, behaviors with places and people. Once they're set, they're hard to break, and maybe never really broken - just fought-off.

It looks like many things have come out of me lately, evolved, except our relationship. I do feel this pressure to stay in contact with you every day, but maybe when it comes down to it, I feel like you're just an impressive guy who knows a lot about me. You were there when I was born, and some of those first 10 years, none of the following 10, and made a few appearances in the last two or three.

Dad?

You're just a guy that I see less than I talk to, less than I can remember you. You're full of advice and we literally share at least half a brain, so you can understand and explain my thinking. It's invaluable; however, it's a resource. You're a resource. Our relationship is a resource.

Maybe I'm too young to understand yet. Maybe I'm confused or hurt or angry; I don't know, but you're distant and I don't know if I even care for it to change. But I do know I'm tired of feeling like I'm supposed to feel something, and something like that isn't easy to tell someone, especially my father, even more so when I know he wants something more.

00:01 AM

Retreat
02052014

Rotating and rambling
They grasp at the ground
Crunching and creeping
As they spin round and round
Tethered to rod
Rusted, crusted, enduring

Its strength is reliant
On small parts securing
A linchpin, like keystone
Fulcrum folly collapse

Infused in its body
It refuses to snap
Floating around on clouds
Air trapped inside rubber

Muffle, cough, hiccup, choke
Sputter, then mutter
Hum under creak
Screech clumber ska-dish

Bones need to stretch
Crack, scratch, itch
Fluids leak from every
Pore and hole they can find

Crotchety crawls leave behind
Trails of slime
Don't stop locomotion
Lest lethargy lock into laze

Be there in a minute
Mechanizes into days
A small spot of oil
Drips onto the floor

Falling short of futile
Effort to fly from the door
Though floating on clouds
Wings no longer flap

Not even firm gliding
Instead, they just crack
A single slam will not suffice
To seal the egress

Again and again
It is pounded and pressed
Repair or replacement of parts
Only reveals

Further misalignment malfunction
Short-circuit and squeal
Never thought things would
Bend-up and end-up like this

Mindless Doodles Make for Mind-Numbing Distractions
02052014

Fog fingers finesse frolicking friends
Whilst wound-down winds wonder when
The thunder thinks thoroughly through thwack-acking
My moon makes mournful music mustering moods
Sun sleeps silently, stomach-down, snuggling stars
Coastlines cuddle crests crashing calmly costing curdles
Grasses greenen greatly, gulping glacier ghosts
Sepia static softens surreptitious sensations
Ink insulates intrinsic insidiousness in ignorant introverts

Silhouettes of Summer
02082014

She wanted something to be lost in the love of the womb
A Diet Cherry 7-Up to drink and red balloon to fly away
She floated through orange sherbet skies
An eternal sunset that never dies
The fizzy bubbles in her mouth
Rose up to add red blush to the clouds
She lost the same last baby tooth and let it drift to the ground
When it clicked and bounced on marble floors below
It chipped and made a sound
A symphony of growing up could be heard for miles around
Her eyes squinted over smiling cheeks
As that same baby tooth moved down
Asail forever in pastel rainbows
The days of her life never passed her by
She never frowned nor wondered why
Just cheerily bobbed through the skies
One day, perhaps, her red balloon will fade
And she will sink down to the shores to promenade
With glee and grace, she will sing to ivory oceans
As the sun tucks away
She will not be frightened by adolescent nights
Make friends with the stars and stare in delight
The novelty of all-new adventures to come will distract from
The pain of her last adult tooth poking out from the gum
Though teeth are swallowed and balloons float away
Red fizzy drinks go flat and the sun hides away
All is not lost from illustrious youth
Pastel rainbows smile high above
Just for you

There is No Original Content, Only Structural Innovation
02092014

Cigarettes and glass pieces
Make nonsense a mess
Jokes dabble inside and out
Hit or miss
Accents create worlds of insanity blessed
By the presence of presents
And pretense of scribbles
Dadulate inside momulators
Instigate outside gators
Exfoliate the faux-lickles
Tickles my fancy fur coat
Barter harder tartar sauce
Lemon wedge on the edge
Of a glasses wetted down by
The bay watermelon is a felon
For selling an ounce by the pint
A wee tad of an ox, orthodox
Churchly steeples and sheep
Weep loudly and proudly without the
Need for help me S.O.S. in a coded
Ring on my finger, you wanker, ligament
Bends and stretches my regret is mine to keep

Visualizer
02172014

Pink pen wrapped in flesh
Ears bundled in vinyl
Desk under two hooves
Screen laced in lines of color contrast
Cord slung into computer
From the side of my face
Formatted thoughts litter a page
Words of wisdom kick eardrums
1.5 liters of air sits on the water
Paper melting pot spills from shoulder bag
Alien abstractions undulate into irises
Ball of alliteration bound by my ankle
It can't escape me
I hold it captive
Wad of observations crumpled under my thumb
Reflections embossed on the next page
Right to left
Creativity crosses hemispheres
Wrinkles into logic
I hold my hand in my palm
Read the creases
Tear the seams
I fold
The color bleeds
Beyond borders
Across the cuts
Every edge is muddled
Contact
Imbued with continuity

Sonder Love
02182014

       Spend a few moments observing every passerby. Try not to judge. Imagine falling in love with them. Find an immediate quality about them that would strike as love at first sight. Transcend the physical. Sex. Read them and discover a defining characteristic which is their greatest strength, as well as their greatest weakness. Understand how it came to be, why it is so, and accept it completely. Be unconditionally in love with them for those few moments.

       See each person who passes through your life, see the rest of your lives together, and let love flash through your mind for an instant, then let it go. They never know. You watch each true love become a part of you and walk away, but you wish them well and grow with each moment.

Teeter Toddler
02242014

Nimble needles flap against blades
Miss the mark
Spiral in
Around
Down
Knees catch the ground
Hair waves goodbye
As spine pulls on the sky
Puffs of breath pant
Pitter patter of cardiac drum
Skin thrums with leg log thumps
Shoulder wings waggle
Finger feathers flap
Gums grab new chewers
Joy folds between eyes and over cheeks
Exertion burdens brow in sweat
Earth takes hold and do-se-do's
Partners swinging round and round
Joining-in
Spinning round and down
Giggle hiccups
Screaming loud

Eruption
02252014

A little bit of smoke
Smoldering sex
Rise
Clouding higher judgement
Tangerine blanket
Mood lighting magma
Ashen perspiration
Oh
Press
Sing
Me

Earth's core alight
I feel the fire
Melting spinal fluid
Suspension bridge
Sway and buckle
Tension escapes in lightning splinters
Until…

Dear Younger Self
03112014

You should be about 13 if you're reading this. I'm 22, looking out on a beautiful day. You are receiving this letter because there are times when you are going to be given very good advice, but you don't take it because you think you know better or think you should find out for yourself, the hard way. A smart man learns from his own mistakes, but a wise man learns from the mistakes of others. You are extremely sensible. You have an instinct and an intuition which is the sharpest of anyone I know. Adolescence was a rough and lonely ride for me, you can do better. Get to know yourself, trust yourself, and treat yourself as kindly as you treat others. Take an interest in others and let positive influences in. Spend time with them. Be open about your affections. Trust me, you will be rewarded and surprised again and again.

Well, that's about the gist of it. Open ears, open heart, open mind. I don't want to dedicate this whole letter to advice, though. This is a rare opportunity. A little 411 on your future self: you are a badass drummer, signature artist, and one hell of a lover.

Sincerely,
22

P.S. Brush your teeth, boy.
10:44 AM

Satori
04272014

       Awoken by the clacking wood of sandals and floorboards. Symphony of bamboo dancing in a gust. Unfolded garb between heartbeats and breath of each air released from the cloth. Cradled sleeve while pouring tea. Whispered story through gurgle and froth. Lost in a sip, the warm cup against fingertips - another call from clattering bamboo stalks. Sword sings, unsheathed and resonating awake. One hundred thirty-six muscles lock into place as first position takes hold. Sweat-outlined stance, awaiting the next movement to flow outward. One breath. One strike. Candle flame extinguished by swipe of steel, returned to rest in sheathe to dream of its next awakening. Fox in the woods stalks through stalks of bamboo. Paper walls flex to changing air pressure. A trace of cherry blossom wafts inside. The smell tells of a coming bloom.

Isolated Validation
04232014

You are not the only one
You are not the lonely one

In the same situation
With the same problem
You are not invalidated
You are invaluable
Dated: April 23, 2014 01:14 AM

You woke up from a dream
Make your dreams your reality
You must continue to be strong
You must be willing to be wrong
Drop your walls and walk outside
Life is a journey, enjoy the ride

You are not the only one
You are not the lonely one

2,000 Points Under the NASDAQ
07072014

The iGeneration
The McGeneration
The Y-Generation
The Hyperbolic Generation
The Atomic Generation
The Cloud Generation
The War on the Middle East
Blu-Ray
IMAX
Fiber Optics
Candy Crush
The Smartphone Generation
Beats by Dre
Wikipedia
Google
Starbucks
Game of Thrones
Hulu and Netflix
Youtube
9/11
Silicone Bracelets
The Red Bull Space Jump
The Cancer Generation
Laptops
Voyager Satellite Going Intergalactic
Breaking Bad
Octomom
Twitter and Instagram
The Facebook Generation
The Internet Generation
Likes Posts Shares Tweets Tumbles
$4 a gallon gas
Blackberry BBM
Going Green
BP Oil Spill
Katrina
A generation underlined and underwritten
Labeled and blamed
How many terrorists did your Avocado Toast profits feed today?

Reflections on Volume V

Halfway through our journey! You made it! Isn't this fun? What's going to happen next? Could be anything, right? Maybe I got hit by a car and I recorded all my thoughts retroactively from dreams after I woke up from a five-year coma, or maybe I finally found true love and retired on the income from inventing the next "pet rock." Yeah, I don't know. Your guess is as good as mine.

"What Are You Doing for Others" holds monumental importance to me. It's a second chance at love! I was 22 in 2014. A girl pursued me during our first year of New College, and I couldn't figure out why (I was still working on the self-love and self-worth thing; didn't make much sense why a girl would actually be so interested in me). I said to myself, "This girl sees something in me, and she is damned determined to be a part of my life. I need to give her a chance to show me what it is, and maybe I can see it, too." Selfish, I know. Don't worry, I liked her a bunch, which eventually grew into more love than I was able to handle. It was the linchpin in the crux of a dam made of my trust issues. We both had pet snakes, so we figured we should probably date each other. With her love, I was *finally* able to move past that old guard—at least for a while—and experience what a mostly healthy and supportive relationship feels like. I say mostly because she held me and my "I don't give a fuck" attitude on a pedestal, and I relied on her to take care of me better than I was taking care of myself.

I spent some time here looking back on my relationship with my father. I started to work on forgiving him for the past and seeking to understand where he was coming from. We were working on talking more regularly, since we had two opportunities to see each other in person for periods of time about as long as all our previous time put together.

I started to engage in some of that intentional positive self-talk. I was unable to "unsee" the critic in my head. More and more, I talked to myself, caught myself saying things I wouldn't even say to people I hated, and actively tried to reframe how I saw myself.

I want to highlight that although I was building a new self-perception and making more important decisions about my direction in life, darkness was not lost on me. I see this volume as a time of forming a healthier relationship with darkness such that I could co-exist with it, instead of being consumed by it. Writing long-ass essays and all this rediscovering love and whatnot got my creative juices flowing, resulting in several short stories and more intricate creative pieces that required more dedication than the occasional passing poem, journal entry, or letter. I believe some of these pieces helped cultivate some of that positive relationship with darkness, harnessing its ruminative and visceral power to craft a more refined voice and build confidence through taking on new territory.

Don't fret! These relationships with lovers, parents, self, and darkness are *working relationships*, and far from clean. Let's get messy.

Our problems do not define us
But how we deal with them

Small successes
Make for great triumphs//

Volume ///VI///

Not Quite 76 Trombones

08132014 /

/ 01192015

Ages 22 - 23

A Cannibal's Heart
08132014

A storm rolls into the room
Through her window as she blows out of town
But a twangy guitar sings my hurt
My heart is hungry

Lightning speaks in thunderous, lunderous lulls
Against the wall, shadows crease here and again
The afterthought is me
Once upon a knife
Could she take that weapon and turn it upon herself?
Inside?
To find the scorpion's flight
The window tears in two

I could only hope
Would she know what to do?
How could our hearts collide again?
Living nerve endings rub to set dead alight again
Lighting flash upon the smile
Lips curl around the blade
An apparition is seen and fades
I grasp at a sound that ripples away

Bliss befolly shrouds incision
Eyes lift open
Consequential decision
Outside lies and lies beyond
Dare not lift the spell
Nor welcome the storm

Cerebral clouds pour venom down panes of glass
Silicate stinger cuts out the last laugh
Cringing boxes of midnight oil
Tousled trunks of locks and keys
Matching games are mortal play dismayed by iron

Shallow circle of hell
The floor depresses under attention
Diverted gaze and glare
Mishappened happiness imagined as a demon's smile

A reflection
Light
Rumble
Hunger
Hurt
Taste

Melodepression
08302014

Quite...how does that make you feel?

Like a loser. Unprepared, passive, inactionable, alone, non-interesting, isolated, unlikable, boring, miserable, restless, anxious, immature, defeated, sad, hopeless, good for nothing, unmotivated, childish, lifeless, burdensome.

It makes me feel like I am nothing, surrounded by nothing, with nothing ahead of me and nothing to add - only to subtract from others, as a parasite, looking for something to be as those around me have so much of something that I may take just a piece and know what it is like to exist in some existence and fall back on the fact that—if nothing else—at least I am, instead of nothing at all.

But so terrible is this wretched lechery to me, my hatred of the act only enables my empty nothingness to grow and grow until all of anything and everything shrinks into a piece that all of eternity and infinity would be required to compute its ever-decreasing value, like the remainder of pi, or the volume of a black hole. What is happiness but an island opposite the meager nothing I demount to? Cast others away by the expanding sea of nothing between. IT MAKES ME FEEL MELODRAMATIC. But if I pretend to be happy, *if* I pretend to be as I am not, I will become as naught, I am. And this set of worries and unhappiness shall be shed, and for the exciting newness of being something other than I was, I will be elated...for a time...until eventually a new set of woes arises in this new self, new malcontents and unfairness, the likes of which I have not faced before, and with this, I am ill-equipped to cope. Further, I will spiral down into a pit of despair whose bottom is a strange mistress with depths beyond my former discouragement. And so, I will yearn for the former—knowing I can never go back—and see the latter, the newer, the unknown elation of a stranger...self.

In the Throes
08302014

Kyle B, Matt C, Constantine D

[[E, G, C, Bm]]

I am rotting in this heat
In this heat
I expire timely in my place
My entire being begins to
Decay and decompose

I'm in the throes
I'm in the throes
I'm in the throes
In your throat

I am eating my eyeball raisins
Festerly feeding on my own tongue
I am rotting and racing the maggots
Eat myself and I am well

Are you well?
Oh well well well
Are we here?
(Are we here?)
Nest for amends
Running mirror
Feeding moon
Trickling taste of love
Killing smooth
Folded pastures
Of wrinkling breath and blood

Sea for yourself
Just come
(These days erasing)
Until you capsize inside your head
And it all turns back again
And you're lost until you live
And the love, there is no love
And I can hear
These days are aging
Ah - love…
(And we all)
(Until you)
Love…
There is no love

Raging of the Elements
09012014

Listen like a lullaby
Listen to me
The cat's scratching our initials
Into the tree

A branch bows down
Swats her to the ground
Sap bubbles out
It's a raging of the elements

Against the storm of awe
I draw my sword of calm
Slash Slash Swish Stab
The growth comes tumbling down

I cradle my Kat
As she licks her wounds
Living in a house
Of timber and wood

I'm peeing in the pond
Over back of the yard
Little bittle ripplin'
Surges into a wave
It sucks me down
The lights go out
It's a raging of the elements

Against the storm of awe
She draws her bow of calm
Slick Quiver Snap Boom
The tide subsides and spits me out

My Kat dries me down
Cozied up to the fire
The stage is set now
For daring devil desire

As sparks ignite
they catch aflame
As passion burns
So does the flame
Trusses collapse
The embers attack
It's a raging of the elements

Against the storm of awe
I fill my glass of calm
Splish Splash Glug Crash
The light smolders Silent Into That
Good Night

Settles in with a blade of cold
We're building up a shelter
Of earth, water, and wood
My Kat and I nestle together
And we hear a rumble
Everything we've worked for
Crumbles, tumbles, and fumbles
The mud contorts
A giant form
It's a raging of the elements

Against the storm of awe
We draw our minds in calm
Bow Spark Swoosh Burn
The giant reduced to a drop from a
cloud

Dear Thesis
09012014

    Good morning, Thesis! Another day and I still don't know exactly who you are. I have some impressions and ideas but nothing definitive. I suppose it's my own fault; I have spent more time and energy avoiding you than getting to know you, which is absurd. We're supposed to be partners this year - friends, even! You could be my best friend, as interesting as I want, all I would have to do is make you as such. But I'm judging a book by its cover. I'm forming my own impression of you based on others' experiences of you. It's not fair to you, but honestly, it just doesn't seem like I'm interested in the things you're interested in: reading, empirical research, pointless publications, APA guidelines, bibliographies, statistics, data analysis, graphs, the list goes on and these are all things I despise. Sure, we might have some similar topics of interest: psychology, working with people, organizing, challenging the ideas of others, presenting our own ideas, arguing their validity and imagining applicability - but Thesis, you and I operate in very different ways and I fear we may be too different of people to get along, and I don't want to get hurt, Thesis! Not like the others: finals, midterms, article summaries, research proposals - all of them ended in emotional disaster, no matter how many times we got back together. I'm scared, Thesis. You have a reputation for being bigger and badder than any other essay I've been with so far and - although collectively - I've handled worse, never have I been with one single such assignment as yourself. Though thousands have succeeded and few failed with you, I'm just...I'm just scared. You. Scare. Me.

    But the fact remains: I must be with you if I am to graduate New College with my Bachelor of Arts in Psychology. We must find a way to coexist, to get along, to get to know each other and be proud of what we have accomplished when this time is over. It is still early in the year, yet. I hope for the best and expect the worst.

    Regards,
    Constantine D.

PARVAN
09082014

Group Writing Game

Pronoun
Article
Random
Verb
Adjective
Noun

One person starts by writing one Pronoun, one Article, one Random word, one Verb, one Adjective, and one Noun. Each word is written in random places on the page. Then, pass it to the next person to do the same. Continue to rotate until the page is filled or the message feels complete.

Ode to PARVAN
09082014

Sleet key celebration
Mean unloved in anguish
Buy fraught blue gall
Time sleeping so near
This is vicious
Gray nor cowardly
Pinewood norms
Piss God off
Defend the relics
Come to fret - Oh!
The way I lie
Manned thirty is with rusting
Crest spacial leeway new
Stoop his doubt
This claw first bell in the looney purse
Monsoon see (me)
Homeward ducks
Eye blink I thirst brought felon
Due crumb serious bubble
Flossed
Pass the tape
Bribe syrup

Letters to Chaos
09082014

Write here
Flight now
List is all I no
Mit
Leave a moment two
Unsettle fist
Bet it gun
Or fret on with lips
At slut bra still
The hurled begun
Bun with legislature
Cat mutt lime still see
Blob and drink
Retort me back
Fi brought miss
Savory nun
Lust
Bomb
Noun

Wednesday
09172014

Here
Wednesday
Middle of everything
Centrally located
The view is
Panoramic
Retrospect
Is only a half turn
From speculation
This wedding's day
Stretch your arms
And spin
From a mountain top
Down
To the
Week's end days

The Poet Tree
09232014

What is the price of poetry?
What is the economy of inflated
meaning?
The narrow nature of supply and
demonstration depleting the
resources of rhetoric

Question
Mark, for the sake of argument

Say that the cost is lost, and we
poets are left to
Barter
Banter
And batter each other with words of
Intellect
Simile
And assimilation

Mark met a four-dollar poet, once

Mark, a litter-rated garbage poet,
himself
Once questioned
Just
Justin
Justin Four Dollar

Mark questioned
Just in four dollars
How did you become so valuable?
To the scene?
To poetry?
Look at me
I am just...
A mark

"Just a mark?" Justin remarked
A Questioning Mark!
Once, I met a mark that merely
Exclaimed!
And I found his droll to be lame,
untame
So emotionally unrestrained that I
could refrain from
Punctuating.
Him.
To the point of no reserve

And in return, justice was served
In just four pence

"Just a mark?" Remarked Justin
My four pence grew to four dollars
Thanks to you

And in just four dollars, Justin Four
Dollars became valuable
The gold standard of the Poet Tree

Thanks to you
A Questioning Mark
With inquisitive, critical eyes
Do not criticize yourself

Thanks to you, Question Mark
In just four dollars, I overcame
blind exclamation
I discovered and disrobed what was
covering up
What I knew deep down

Thanks to you
I know my value
I owe you a debt so great
You are not worthless
You are, without question, Mark,
invaluable

96

Other Day
09272014

Yesterday
Monotony woke me
With nothing other than what I expected
The bed creaked as it rolled me off
Winding up my spinal spring
Ticking coiled mechanical joints
Stiff, rusting rain of every day

Sunglasses
The same tinted sun
Conditioned air
Unaltered stone steps
Checkpoint doorways
Until

Oily spontaneity doused my overwound clock
Time fell away
Minutes turned to the days of our lives
And hours of something new
Softened to sinews threaded in the moment

Shaken
I stirred
Mixing in
Breaking the ice
Full to the brim
Joy overflowed
Fresh mint mingle
Cocktail conversation
Salty sarcasm splashed on the rocks
Twist of a line
At the bottom of a bottle
Leaves a lipstick mark
On napkin nights
Bubble intrigue rises to the surface
Pops politely
Fizzles
Sizzles
Dribbles over the edge
Slides down the line
Lands in hand
Turns to decide
How old is the night?

Dark Water
09282014

I am a ship
My mast is tall
And I am setting sail
Into the blissful abyss

Florida
09312014

Lotta bugs
Lotta stagnant water
Lotta little itches and bites needing to be scratched
Lotta rain
Inconsistent
On and off
Sun is shining
Rain is pouring
Sun is shining
Rain is pouring
Passing by
Coming
Going
Waiting
Lotta wishless ambitiousness
Lotta senseless need to protest
Lotta rebellion to what we know
Lotta concerning with matters insignificant
Lotta lack of the flow to go with

Water sitting

So it shows that
My reflection
Calm and serene
Swollen with infectious histamine
Larvae writhing beneath my skin
This small puddle we live in
Tiny creatures in an ocean
Take out my anti-itching potion
Spongey earth
Even grass is full of rain and itching afterbirth
Drowning silent beneath my feet
Tiny ripples between trimmed blades
The browning sun comes cooking down
Bug bites are rising through the burned and blistered sun-kissed skin
Fingernails are dragging blood

Inertia
10012014

A bit bored
Settled
Complacent
No longer new
Symptom of youth, of living

Searching for stimuli
For excitement
The newest
The unknown
The dangerous
The extremity

It needs ups and downs to have a wavelength
A pulse
Things begin to settle
Make a splash
Throw a wrench in the plans
Shake things up
Or
Just write about it and hope that sinking feeling falls away and you will magically
float to the surface

Hope that putting it into words
Someway
Somehow
That externalizing it will make it separate from you
And you can move on
Move away from it

Just write or talk or think about it
Then try to ignore it and push it away
Or just DO something
Anything real enough to say that you tried
Started
Ventured
Branched-out
Got off your sinking, sulking ass and did something about it

Acknowledge
Act
Follow through
Reflect

Borrowed Youth
10072014

      Sitting in front of the cafeteria as a front makes itself known above. A plate of food is prepared for the many, no effort on my part. Friends, acquaintances, and friendly strangers come and go between mouthfuls.

      I chew on the idea that this is as good as it gets. No bills, kids, or quotas. Freedom of expression. Intellectuals and institutionally-informed opinions everywhere, united via individuality. Roofs over our heads, clothes on our backs, an abundance of food and always something to do. Opportunities to travel and pursue our passions on someone else's dollar, no effort on our part, everything is just handed to us.

      In that, it is not meant to last.

      It is intended to be transcended.

Turns & Burns
10152014

I gotta let you love me
I gotta let you please me
I gotta let you need me
Oh baby, don't you tease me

Now if you don't release me and burn
Oh babe
If you don't leave me now
We're gonna crash and burn
Lovely lady
Better hit the road
Or these wheels won't turn

We tried everything we had to give
We just gotta let on, get out, and let live
Cuz girl, I got love for you
But this won't work

Oh, girl, I want bad for you
But together we're worse
We just hope for the best, baby
And plan for the worst

So if you still got love, baby
Best take it with you in your purse

Clench
10152014

There
In your hand
Is a microphone
On an epiderm stand

Scream
All the rage inside of you
And cry, cry, cry
All the bad I done

It's one more tear
In the shotgun
A .45 caliber crystalline drop
A fully-automated salt stream

Down on your knees
Baby, you're cocked and loaded
Directing your aggression
At targets unseen

But I'm the one
Oh, all the bad I done
The taste of bad blood covers your gums
And the gun fires away

A Means to Amends
10152014

Oh, honey
You been walking in my thoughts
I been wondering about you
But the time has come
To kick off your shoes

I tried to be honest
(I) Tried to be true
But if the truth hurts
I guess I only done wrong by you

In the end
I guess my feelings
Were lost on you

In the end
Good things are better
When we don't have to pretend

Cascade
10172014

See how slow they move
Against a backdrop of blue
Not a care
Not a worry
Not in the least troubled

See how they lean
With little nails of green
Not a thought
Nor concern
Seasons shed their summer hairs

Hear it stride from limb to limb
Sliding through each small divide
No matter
Never mind
Cannot be seen
But does not hide

Feel its long, massaging arms
Kissing each uncovered pore
Bring the scent of wild love
Pouring over from above

Smell its presence
Fill your lungs
Cleansing rush of new and fresh

Waves of tidal change in turn
Simply flowing, unconcerned
Bare the blooms to naked limbs
Float them slowly to the floor

Here I lay and here I see
Here I feel and here I breathe
Always thinking, never know
Changing as the seasons go

American Culture
10182014

For 300 years
The United States has been in conflict
Domestic for a short time
Surrounded by international wars
United we stand
But it has ever been
United against a common enemy

Afraid if we
Divide from conflict
We will fall

It's time to evolve
Time to resolve
To acknowledge common humanity
And unite across dividing lines
Without erasing cultural divides

Something to Rely On
10272014

Over and over again
It's the same story
In a different pair of shoes

Walk with me as we talk
About the places we've been
Different faces and scenes

Figuring life out
On a case-by-case basis
Trying to relate to this or that

The hats we wear and trade
Betrayed or elated
Some degraded
Faded in this light

A sense of right and wrong
We're all just getting along
Together or alone

We get hurt and we heal
So long as we feel
It's something to rely on

It's something to hold on to
Through drips and drops
As things evolve

Hold onto the old
Or shed for the new
Neither here nor there
Just something to do

Liminal
12092014

The winds are the sweepings of
ghosts passerby
Of gargantuan gusts
Of monolith whirlwinds
Leviathan lulls and humdrum swirls

The dead gather up and slowly
recoil
While the living breathe deeply
Recounter
Recoil

The winds are the sweepings of
ghosts passerby
The mists are the tenuous tears in
their eyes
Mountains are bodies decayed and
compiled

Dust
Mounding
Star-bound
Swept away into derile winds

The winds are the sweepings of
ghosts passerby
Feel their touch
They are calling
They are waiting
They smile
Smile back
They are watching
They are strolling behind
At your back

They are swelling
There they dwell
Not in hell
Nor in heaven
But by and with
For your side
As their ancestors did once
For them
For their trials
For them there is time
There is place

There is presence and moment in
their actions
They assist those still in denial

The wind is the sweepings of ghosts
passerby
Their gentle caress
Undefiled through crevices and
cracks
Those imperfect gaps in between
They lazily lay on leaves in the
trees

Father of Will
Goddess of Love
Ourselves the Creation
The Creators, above

Only Things Left
12102014

I'm a radical
It's about reclamation
Combating cultural appropriation
Gotta promote the left-wing agenda

Not never once inclined
To spend a dollar past a dime
Farmer's markets, thrift shops
Is where I spend my time

Anytime anyone speaks out of line
I jump all up on 'em
Virtual reality
That's right -
Handle all my business passive-
aggressively

My top priority
Is grabbing-up attention
Not down with the mortgage
system
You know I'm livin in a tent
Son!

I get my thrills
Writing tl;dr posts
I got the
Strongest
Loudest
Rowdiest
Power of will

Some peers correct you a little
I correct you the most

Impossibly pretentious
Would be to put it mildly
Far as I'm concerned
I've got limitless abilities

When I'm feelin really tall
I swing my nuts at protests
Demonstrations
Or tagging posters on the streets

The squeaky wheel gets the grease

And ain't nobody greasier than me
We oughta burn it down
Fuck a culturally appropriated
stereotype-reference-promoting
ignoramus discrimination
embedded in traditionalist values

We oughta change everybody's
attitudes
Fuck a thousand-year-old scripture
worshipping a hierarchal patriarchal
power
If it ain't paganism or "spiritual"
They can suck the matriarchy's
dick

Fuck a nation-wide distributor
The only thing I read is DIY 'zines
Fuck takin daily showers
Bitch!
I'm naturally clean

Fuck sexual advances
I didn't consent to you asking me
consent
If you ask me one more time
What I stand for
I'll show you how loud I can shout

Fuck you! Fascist pig!

My generation is the one to make
the social revolution big
Ask me one more time what I give
a shit about
Imma get up in your ear and yell

Everything is relative
Your dogma can go to hell

This Too Shall Pass
12172014

None carry the weight so heavy as this
Bar-none
The ability to drain all your bliss
But this
This too shall pass

As solemn as you may sit or stand
As grave and gruesome as your hand is dealt
And this
This too shall pass

Though the clouds gather
And the flowers wilt
Though silken linens wear bare
And wine stains are absolute
So this
This too shall pass

Yes
Even night turns to day
And day into night
Through bittersweet celebrations and sorrow
This too shall pass

Break Away
12232014

To fly so high
One must not carry weight
One must be free
And unfettered
And feathered in gait

To reach towards the skies
One mustn't be blind
One must see through deception
Like the oracle's all-seeing eye

To scratch at earth's ceiling
One must take in the air
Breathe deeply and calmly
Whilst rising to dare

To soar by the wind
One's reach must be open
To welcome the breeze
And skim over the ocean

To slide without effort
Over columns of thermals
One must seek the comfort
Of flocks warm and eternal

Dumb
12312014

Today I'm feeling dumb. I'm feeling humdrum, like a bum, like one in two instead of one in two million. A villain and vain. I'm feeling black, blank, white, rather plain. I'm feeling disdain for myself and my commonness and participation in the typical scenario of hypersexual primitive predictable over-charged libido. I'm feeling like a fool to myself and taking things way too serious because I'm needy and delirious. Weak and confused, vulnerability-infused, putting myself in positions of power in my mind, but acting weak in words and behaviors, in favors—sexual or otherwise—just looking for a fix. So, I'm twisting context and strangling little slivers of hope, trying to squeeze out every last drop like dope. I'm hiding the truth from myself and others so badly it's a demon-stration of my lack of maturation and my power of manipulation, a sheer lack of patience and some poor justification for how I act, how I attack, and now - how I smack myself around, the way I jump the gun and regret falling down. The way I slam my fist to the floor in horror of what a whore I am just under my skin.

Been acting bottomlessly shallow, a king without a castle with nothing to show for what he claims to be, just a sheath for misery in a miser. I'm none-the-wiser, death defier, short replier, sexual tiger, snake in the grass, Machiavellian ass, inconsiderate and crass, swimming upstream until I'm up the creek, lured by siren's screech, fail to teach myself right from wrong, nowhere to belong, keep repeating to myself over and over that I have to be strong, with two left feet I dance in the street like a deer in the headlights until it's light out and hindsight will show 20 over 20 years living in chains, a victim of circumstance instead of catalyst of change, denying how deranged and estranged I am in my lonely little world, blaming it all on every bit of sadness over a silly little girl, whether this one or that, the heart attack is my own because no one else can get past the cage of ribs that my heart calls home, Stockholm syndrome, I love the pain that I make for myself but still want to break free, instead of questioning the world around, I question everything inside me, unsure of myself in every single step, hesitating forward and back, wincing, cringing, and holding my breath like a scared little boy waiting for all the pain to go away instead of accepting it as part of the play.

Dear K
12312014

I want to say that I do care for you and you are very special to me. I simply cannot believe or get over how good you are to me and how much you care about me and all the things you do for me. It is truly a fantastic demonstration of love.

I want you to be a part of my life. You're more than anyone could ask for, more than any man could ask for. You're smart, loyal, beautiful, caring. Until now, sex is the most enduring part of our relationship, the strongest tie that we come back to and relate best through. We struggle with many things except communication, we are extremely open with one another, but at the same time I feel like I shut you out sometimes, and you shut me out, too.

I feel there are times when you just want to know what's going on with me and I won't let you in, and I feel there are other times where I want to have a very routine, normal conversation with you about things and you hide yourself from me; that lack of confidence bubbles up and I get irritated. It's a struggle. You deflect every invitation to sharing in the conversation as if nothing you have to say is of any value, and I get tired of trying to pull it out of you. There's also a lot of times I go through bouts of just wanting to be left alone and I know that's hard on you, but I feel like I do come back. You feel like the only time I come to you or pay attention to you is when I'm bored, that you're my last resort, that I'm settling on you.

That's it.

I haven't made you feel like you are my first choice and not my last.

I want you to know that simply is not true.

I care so much for you and I think it's something that is growing - especially recently - the more you mature and gain confidence in yourself. I appreciate the great confidence you have in your feelings for me and your dedication. I admire that in you. Ironically, I'm the one that's lacking confidence in that department. I think you are a dream. That is how I see you, as a dream. You have an endless list of wonderful qualities and in our time together, since I've known you, you have acknowledged your shortcomings and worked to overcome them, and that is outstanding. It makes you all the better.

I have not shown you the same love and dedication that you show me.

I am constantly hot and cold with you, but lately, I've been getting warmer. I keep thinking about you and playing this scenario in my head: If you were gone, I know it would be a great loss and a tough time for me to handle. I want us to be together. I want you in my life. I want to have the patience to keep our relationship intact in whatever form is necessary so we can continue to help each other and be there for each other. I don't know if I have been there for you as you have been for me, though. I hope I have, and I hope that you feel like I have, too. I want to be as good to you as you are to me, but you make it a tough race, haha.

GOD, you're gorgeous. You have so much going for you. I know you're going to be alright and do great, and great things will come to you. I think you're starting to see that, yourself. I see an adventurousness and confidence growing in you, and that's what I want the most. You have to grow out of your awkward phase and have confidence in yourself, and I have to grow out of my self-centered phase and have patience with others. I want you to have the confidence to keep me in check when I'm being an ass, to keep me in line. I want to have the tolerance and love for you which will nurture you and help you grow, to feel loved and supported.

I want you to know that you have given me so, so much in such a short time. You have shown me—at the very least—what my wildest dream for a companion could be. I appreciate you and all that you do, have done, and will do. You are so very special to me, and what is past shall remain forever a special place in my heart. There is no reversing that, and because of the light you've brought me, I want to be there for you for whatever and whenever you need.

I want you to know that you're not perfect.

I want you to know that I'm not perfect.

I want you to know that it's okay to be insecure or feel less-than sometimes, but that does not define you.

I want you to know that as long as you can make someone else feel loved, you will never be unloved, but in order to do that you have to love yourself, first. Flaws and all.

I want you to know that your love is not in vain.

I want you to know that you absolutely rock my world and you are my first choice, and anyone who doesn't line up for you is a damn-ed fool.

Fear of Losing You
12312014

Yes, that's part of it
But
Do not define the whole of love by
its part
Acknowledge the way you feel
when
You think about her, talk to her,
touch her

Acknowledge the smile she puts on
your face
Accept the love she has for you
Accept the love she has for you
Accept the love she has for you

The roles have been reversed from
the last
Do not be a victim of your past
Do not make those same mistakes
Accept the love you have for her

Look at all the parts of your
affection for her
Stop getting tunnel vision on the
superficial ones
Examine how your love runs deeper
Be bold!

Do not deny thy love
Swallow it up and rise above
Follow the magnetic north of your
heart
Learn from your mistakes

Look back on your chart
Do not give way to fear of the
known
Live better and alight
Where darkness has shown

Be true your intentions
Shed not the self-lie
Lest your compass lose focus
Tricked to follow true north
Misdirected by the wily mind
Urging forward in motion but
gravely off course

Beware the sirens of sex and the
tides of temptation
When you've lost all direction let
the whales lead the way
Their great hearts and slight songs
keep the sea devils at bay
Whisk away from the whirlpools
which take you down in a spin
Play the harp of your heartstrings to
stay attuned what's within
And when they're in the wrong key
you must listen more closely
That ship may have sailed, a new
bay be more homely

Remember there's all different
sailors at sea
Some forever stay searching, in
love with adventure
Some tie up their sails when they
find what they treasure
Whatever it be that you ask of the
world - remember

The sea is an oyster and sailors are
pearls
If it didn't last
Just be glad you fell in love with a
girl

Turn of Phrase
01132015

This world is one sentence
A multitude of sounds
Of letters
Of meanings
Intonation produced incantation
Spellbound creation
Confined by its initiation to
punctuation

It is no more than when it is said at
pace with all others
Passing into the historical abyss

This world is one sentence
As a man may call a dog
As a child may inquire in futility
As a woman may comment on the
day

This world is but a sentence
It too shall pass away

A mote of dust among the others
Gently blowing in the breeze
So very like it
Yet starkly different
Save a stressed syllable or phrase

This world is but a sentence
Which may be spoken by one soul
For all souls on earth
Such other worlds untold

One passing conversation
A greeting, goodbye
All life to death
Begins and ends so many times and
turn forever
Turn of phrase

For all the letters and words
combined with so many speakers
For they whom spellbind
One flees and endless others exist

This world is but a sentence
For every one that stands
Countless others stand beside

For every mouth that utters
So many others speak and cry

A passing thought
A minor whim
All and all
Contained within

A slighted sigh
Give cosmic pause
One second thought
Is all that ever was

This world is but a sentence
Just a line of but a page
Of a chapter
Of a book
Of volumes
On a shelf
One of sundry archival sage

One word could be the beginning
Or the end
Beware what you say

Heritage Prayer
01192015

Things fall apart
The future is out there
It is only a matter of time
Undoubtedly, manifest destiny continues
May we come in peace
Though the blood of the past is on our hands
Though we have arrived
Our vainglorious hour
Through utility forget we not that which makes us human
Our capacity for both great love and great evil
Let us not forget solidarity of all existence and our place in it
Let history be merciful and the future promise more
Let every moment be the present and in that moment be there
Love
Light
Life

Reflections on Volume VI

"Not Quite 76 Trombones" takes place from 2014 to 2015; I was 23 years old. Things were going too well. Time to get messy again.

It was senior thesis time, and I had learned long before (well, 5 years before this) when I aged out of scouts at 18—before I finished my Eagle Project—that done is better than nothing at all. I found out about self-compassion as a psychological theory, and it was right in line with everything I'd been working on during the past year or two. It was new enough that its research base consisted of only about 100 studies, and they were all freely accessible from a single website. In short, a thesis student's wet dream. At the time, same-sex marriage was gaining heat in the press as it blazed from state to state and started heating the federal legislative pot to a boil. I was attending a school with an unusually high representation of LGBTQ+ students. Interesting and exciting stuff. Opportune, you might say. I decided to stand up, speak out, and conduct a research study on "Self-Compassion in LGBTQIA+ Individuals." Some people were not appreciative of my initiative, shouting over the internet that cis-hetero, mesomorphic, middle-class, white males like myself needed to sit down and shut up, and understandably so; Constantines like myself had had a bad rep ever since that one asshole in 342 BCE introduced the first-ever law against homosexuality. My namesake was on the line and the U.S. government was on the verge of saying, "It's okay to be gay" to the world. I had no choice but to take action.

Writing a 115-page thesis while many people are shouting at you over the internet in a tiny liberal arts college that your thesis is wrong, your views are wrong, and your existence is wrong, is hard. Thankfully, I had a lover to support me through this difficult and trying time. Unfortunately, I was a very particular and head-strong person who was used to being solo and being hurt. My demons came back to whisper things into my subconscious. My patience wore thin. I started nitpicking and distancing myself.

About halfway through this volume, I decided the relationship was a bad idea because it didn't feel fair to either of us for me to have any doubts while she was so sure. I broke her heart, then we got back together. I got accepted to an AmeriCorps program with City Year in Denver, CO. I passed my dissertation for my thesis. I graduated with my Bachelor of Arts in Psychology. She stayed with me that summer, then I broke her heart again.

Are we noticing some patterns yet? Maybe some unsettled personal work? Doubt. Grief. Pity. Perfectionism. Comparing. Screw it, I jumped back into a shame cycle and started plowing forward once more in the pursuit of change and achievement. There is no success or failure, only in being satisfied with what you have done, are doing, and will do.

The sea sings my sorrow
May the mountains lift me up//

Volume

///VII////

Hello, My Name Is

01202015 // 06032016

Ages 23 - 24

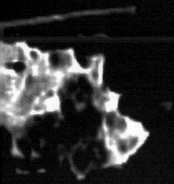

Paraloids Of Of (A New College Collaboration)
02042015

cookie paraloids and polaroid
lullabies
photography maps observations
cyanotype sculptures
you goal section contracts from
the personal style manifestos
nail machines misunderstood codes
of interactive doodles
your favorite fortune actually needs
to learn algebra

misunderstandings
knitting tweets to past and future
selves
simple revivals
choose your last piano and test wills
tell exchanges to understand them
essays
essays
essays
professor playlists
oppression fighting thoughts on
childhood stories for scripts
modern-day adaptations of security
cards to social diagrams
#ootd
asmr
aments
chants
things that make you cry
letters own patterns
unacademic screeds model utopias
academic comics rate my entries
screenshots
of,
of,
of,,,
or
you've forgotten word clusters
book and pieces contour prepared
photobombs
made up wills
prepared fortunes

protest confessions
simple technologies with your silent
commentary

conversations from the last ideas on
the meaning of life

recommendations for your
ultrasounds: email slow exchanges

with lost creative heresies
stop uncles cootie motion with your
mom
you
you 8-year-old
he actually films creepy, moving
reactions to (see) instructions
and constructed late-night videos
and tutorials about how he
guides
email exchanges with lost condom
brothers

misunderstandings of how figures
break-up
favorite OKCupid entries
word art jams
crossword self-care routines
tarot card selfies
casual transcriptions of translations
of puzzles of transcripts that
became manuscripts lost on
facebook email texts adventuress
papeles picados

microficitions atheist

policy memos about the beauty of
nature
cyphers had dreams
humorous art exchanges with music
reviews
sketches
drunk horoscopes output
lists
stories stories
poems poems
songs
art
road trip epiphanies
poltergeists infomercials contracts
recipes

bellybutton monies
lint pastas
journal pastiches

acrostic church dances yet
grandparents
biblical erasures want prayers
parodies of night coasters
we all share brother counters
coasters (the memories forms
videos) all coasters

Minimalism
02192015

Juxtapose
It's just a pose
Nothing more
Something less

Adjacent debates
Counter repose and reposite
These two don't fit together
Three's a crowd of interference
Clouded inference

Minimalism appears and fades
In an effort to overcome itself

Higher resolution and faster shutters reveal
There is something still to dissect
Frames of movement
Of motion

Still of what was once in motion
Frozen in a frame
Thawed by the imagination
Reconsidered back into action

There is more to be said
But commentary is reduced to a wave
Sine waves represented by sign language
The silence is deafening

These many things are imported from the furthest corners of one's imagination
With two or three more
They're encompassing new lands
Waterfalls into desert sands

What does it mean?
What other meanings hide behind these overtly presented archetypes?
In the middle-distance
Minimalism struggles with itself

The closer you look
The smaller it gets
Soften your gaze
Look more closely

Boys & Girls
05112015

I know society's got you squeezed into those tight jeans
Feeling like you ain't something
If you ain't showing something
Clearly, it's hard not to obsess
Over the way you look
Because you do look so good

But for all the looks you get
Few ever get to see
Past the smokescreen
Of perfume and hairspray
Bras doubled up to fill your bust
Jeans with the high waist
Drawing lines on your face
But you mustn't cry

That's where I step in
With quadricep pecs
And bicep broad chest
Should I ever shed a tear
Or acknowledge another man
Lest I be less than
Or, God forbid
I be labeled as a queer

But enough about me
Let's concentrate on you
Because you're front and center stage
In every single thing you do
The way you walk
The way you talk
The way you breathe
The way you sneeze
If you're lost on how to do these things
Go pick up a magazine
While Cosmo talks about sex
Men's Health will tell you how many reps

Boys and girls
To get respect
Use your body
Love,
Society

Carpet Stains
05052015

Long-since has love disgraced me
Or did I cast the first stone?

Her polished, gleaming eyes
Bite-sized smiling cheeks
I see her from across downtown

Oh, will she come and talk to me?
How many days since that night?
The laundry list of fights outweighs
the
Oh! Oh! Oh!
Calling out each other's names
Flip of the sheets and blame flies
over the bed
The last time was the last time

The sun rays over your crown
Her, lifted on a sea breeze
Down by the bay I see you
And you're no longer with me

The bartender looks so good tonight
In tiny shirt and yoga tights
Something about her makes me
hate the way you
Grab your arms when you're lost in
thought

Fall off the stool
Whiskey puddle on the floor
Reflecting back
And all I see is

Walking up to me
Two glasses in hand
Lost in the green in your eyes
I ask you to repeat your name again

The blood on this knife is warm in
my hand
And beating in the other
Is this your heart or mine?

I left it on the carpet when you
walked away
I turned my back

You twisted the blade
And I put a thorn in your side

Now we're both collecting tears
Comparing the scars we left on
each other
And when we get tired
And doubt swoops in
Pick them up from the floor
Wipe them off
And give each other our lonely,
dirty hearts again

Now I can't remember
Since I've piled so many thoughts
onto that one single memory
Did you shatter our love with that
first stone?
Or was it me?

Ballad of Eldenchild
05152015

Woah, I'm fuckin bored
I ain't got shit to do
All I do all day is sit around

Not enough fuckin time
Too much fuckin time
Time is everywhere and it's wasted
On me
And it's wasted
Like me
And it's wasted
Whiskey
And coke, essential oils, and more whiskey

And who the fuck is calling me now?
Leave me alone
Goddamnit, I'm so alone
Lonely
Bored
Time
Drink
Holy shit
Just wastin' my days
Wastin' away
Delete my search history

Privilege
08092015

Privilege is not having to adapt to a situation because the situation is adapted or will be adapted to you.

Hot, Dry Day
08152015

It felt like his throat was bleeding. He tried to speak but all that came out was a cracked and crispy cough. Someone passed him on the street, smiled, said, "Hello." Even stretching his lips to smile was like tearing canvas over a frame of teeth.

Dry, hot air pumped through the terraced metropolis and reflective windows. Since wandering in only three weeks ago, he wondered if it would be fair to say his voice was stolen instead of lost. Maybe moving here was him giving it up.

She was a girl who knew that about him better than most; he couldn't take the heat. It sucked the juice right out of him. He smiled and remembered how cold she was. Maybe that's what drew him in. He was the one who melted in the end.

Live
09162015

If life is a luxury, then despair is to declare that there is nothing left to look forward to. The living have long but stolen the moments of glory from the dead, all of whom remain in their graves, unfettered and dirt poor - unable to afford even decent soil or exotic flowers. Wreaths of thorns draped 'round head, stones warn against the merits of losing one's head over capital gains.

Instead, pursue the end. Once you've tackled it, the means are rustified and decay by dollars. Walls of water are swimmable only to those who are warm. Again, the cold and dead die again, unable to chisel away at their frozen box. Rocks litter the floor as they toil eternal in search of the first stone, eager to meet its caster and cure the empty apology.

Knowledge is born of a newborn baby. All is new and bright and overwhelming. Tell me, do you remember a time when everything was indistinguishable? Merely a scene to be delighted in. A play put on and delivered just for you, and slowly, as you matured, the responsibility fell on you. Did the stork who dropped you drop something new? Was it a desire to go backstage and meet the cast and crew? Who knows. That's the answer to the question once asked.

Next thing you knew you abandoned the audience to become part of the cast, and how strange it is to meet pure observers of your play, imagining they too may one day step into your shoes. When their day comes, you may cling to the resentment you grew, every day the more hating life's end you pursue. Unaware of the director you never met. The stork you fantasize would become your pet.

When the curtain calls and all turns black, honors and flowers thrown for the play you put on without a script, handed down from another dead-and-gone. Will you be satisfied with the role you played? Lead monologue or supporting tech?

Open Water
10042015

Sleep's gentle waves pull me away from waking shores
The rhythmic sound of my breathing
Breaks in low bellows
And slows to a thrum
Each pull is smaller
And calmer than the last
I can feel my body
Rolling off the sand
Floating past the breakers
Thoughts of inspired unconscious
A bump over the sandbar makes me blink
I am now in open water
The stars shrink away in the ocean depths
Behind my eyelids

I Fucking Hate Coffee
10042015

2 AM
Another
I buoy to the surface of my sleeping
waters
This time, rafted aloft by another
thought
Worming its way into my
consciousness
I think of the love(s) I've had in my
life
Flings and objects of affection
never fully realized
I imagine meeting them in the
future
And I realize now
It is already several years hence
these loves
The future I once thought of
Of imagining bumping into chance
From the days when those same
loves became fresh heartbreaks
That future from then is now
And I see myself alone or in
between
And I remember youth
Days when elders would assure me
Forever would be more of the same
happy everything
Just fine
All will be provided
And joy will continue to bleed from
every moment
A new discovery
A non-concern
An unquestioning faith

I remember seeing people looking
sad
And thinking
That's sad
I hope they feel better in a minute
Not realizing the potential for an
entire life of sadness
Only bottling their sadness into a
fleeting moment
As if they couldn't have a cookie
and would forget about it as soon as
someone asked them to play

Nowadays
I look around and I see the
possibilities are endless
Truly understand it

And among them not just minutes
But months of despair
Brought on by years of
responsibilities bearing down
Of expectations and being let down
Of tears being wrenched from the
deepest part of my gut
Because no other physical
expression will render any
reassurance
The unutterable, guttural
hopelessness and fear
That when my elders told me that
everything will be just fine
That that
Was... is... just...
They didn't tell me that it's my
responsibility
They didn't tell me about
responsibility so I could understand
what it meant to be responsible for
my own happiness
That was something that fell on
Mom and Dad and Santa and the
Easter Bunny and everyone else
Anyone else
But me

And now I find myself
And now I look for myself
And now I've lost myself
And now
Now I forget what it was to be
happy
I chase dreams of what memories I
think were there
But I'm not sure if I'm just making
it up

I meet an ex in a coffee shop
Sometime in the future
We ask how the other is doing
What the other has been up to

There is an exciting unearthing of
feelings past
I remember emotions I have yet to
forget
And then I realize I have no joy to
share
That my life up to that point is a
series of events gone into thin air

And as my heart bottoms-out
Their significant other walks-up
with two cups of coffee
They apologize for taking so long
Joking
I laugh to be cordial
But they laugh…together
And look at each other
Oh…introductions are made
"Old friends"
Then time creeps back in
Lost before to bright memories
Eclipsed by a silence
And the barista calls my name
And I remember

I fucking hate coffee
Why am I here?
I forget the whole hypothetical
But I'm left with that feeling
Eclipsed by the silence

My eyes start to sting and my
stomach twists
My body tightens in anger
My teeth clench down on failure
And my loneliness outgrows my
physical form
Contorting my soul to make room
for more
I cut my guts open to give them
some air
Tear back the flesh to do the same
for my muscles
I crawl out of my body, escaping
through the nearest window
Leaving the warmth of what
blessings I have
Alone again in ungrateful winter
Sitting for hours or more
Maybe months

Like I'd come to understand the
possibility that I can be sad
I can be depressed
I can end up alone
I can fail
I can unravel
And I am no different from any
other sad man or woman that I have
ever seen

I could be all that they can be
More
Or less
It's up to me
I'm seeing that having so many
things and opportunities and people
They can still amount to nothing
If I decide they don't count
If I don't give them value
If I don't value them
If I don't make
My life
Valuable

Week's Wax
10082015

Come Monday, I try to find my mind again
Come Tuesday, I'm seeing double
Wednesday falls and I'm stuck in the middle
Thursday ain't even there
I'm just waiting for
Come Friday, my candle's burned
Down
Down
Down
Down down down
Down down down
And my head's all full
A week's worth of wax in my ears
Can't hear
Won't hear
Can't hear
Won't hear
No more
Gotta clear my head for the week's end

Season of Youth
10122015

Regardless—and maybe even because of—the challenges I face this year, these are the days I may come to cherish the most in the future. When things become easy and automatic, I will miss the change-battered hardships of youth, and I will wish I could have appreciated the season of youth to its fullest while I had it.

Essence of Romance
10132015

There are many ways to initiate, but romance is the sustenance of relationship, of which there can be none in the absence of intimacy. However, there is no direct causality. One begets the other. Starting a relationship requires suspension of disbelief, maintaining one requires preservation of disbelief.

Will Power
10292015

How can we measure will?
What is will power?
How does it exist within us?
How do we identify it to the point that we can quantify it?
It seems a critical component of—excuse my bravery and vagueness—consciousness.
But how is it different?
How may it be separate?
Is it universally quantifiable?
Is will as simple as the ability to make a choice?
Even simpler: an act of defiance?
Is it a number of choices or disobediences?
Is it the complexity of them?

Can it exist in a vacuum, when there is only the illusion of choice?
We may find answers in how we view organisms with strong versus weak will power.
Is will integral to character?
Or is it a behavior in flux?
Can it be diminished or increased? Is it elastic?
What internal factors determine will?
External?
What are the components of will?
Is it a sum of parts?
Can some be subtracted, substituted, interchanged?

Stiff Joints
10232015

My heart is no less than 2,000 miles away at any given time
I can't see past the horizon
But I can feel the sun beating my back
My total arm's length is 6 feet
I can reach for the nearest safety ring
But the sun beats down
The strain breaks my arm
And I beat back in retaliation
I beat the sun
I beat myself
Up on high
The sun looks down upon me
My elbow still cracks to this day

Insecure
10312015

I am bottled but stretched
Express myself through a slow drip
The inner me

Otherwise
I apply myself in a paste
In a haste
To wear my heart on my sleeve

I wear bare the thread
So thin
The wind can sway me into the sun
Or blow me back under a dark cloud
Spin me up in a twister
Victim to the elements
Shedding straw

If I only had a heart
I could nail it to a cross
Maybe yours
Better off
I don't want the responsibility
I feel
Inability to love

Surrender
Bottle
Stretch
Guarded on guard
Angst-dripping death grip
Around my own pain and pity
Waiting to be happy
Horny all the time
Any heart I have left is down in my pants
Trying to fill a hole in me
By filling holes in someone else

Double Take
11202015

I saw a girl
Some years ago
So far and yet so near

She reached across a thousand miles
And grabbed me by my ear

I gazed upon her
Peered through when shown a light
Now casting shadows
Now I see
The parts previously unknown to me

The light and dark form figure full
No more or less than human

Through grace and gracious glass, I look
Now seeing which parts I mistook

Her learning curves
Her curves to learn
Pursued and pulled and pushed

Detritus
11202015

Beneath the crumbling stump
The roaches roar and chew

I, the leaves beneath the tree
She, the bare limb above

I lay in wait for the day she is ripe for decomposition
And we will join the soil together

Fertility gods of Promethean Spring
Unworshipped skeletons
Decrepit idolatry impressed upon the roots
Absorbed
Absolved

We reach for the sun through sprouting stems
To fall again the winter yon

Declaration
10232015

I want to go forth and enjoy myself. I want to love every minute of this once-in-a-lifetime experience. I want to endure through difficulty and appreciate the opportunity to grow through those challenges. I want to push my limits. I want to change. I want to grow. I want to love. I want peace within. I want to be confident in all that I do. I want to enjoy everything and everyone around me. I want to lift people up. I want to ask for adventure. I will do these things, and I will do them well and I will be alive with these many great accomplishments. And let me not forget that more important than what is written on the page, is what is written on my heart.

White
12182015

White devil, I am
I and I
Wonder bread
Saltine cracker
Chlorine bleach
Whitewash where I glance
Appropriate my heart's content
Gatekeeper of social justice
Holder of all that is current
Clinging to past oppression
Equality is progressive
Ahead of my time
Make that…ours
What's yours is mine
What's mine will be in a landfill by
Tuesday

Cis-hetero white male
I made the system
I can't fail
Earth's racial minority
Top 1%
Top priority

Ethnic drainage
Sell it back to you
Messiah come
I am
Man
Impregnate you and force you to
keep it
Raise it
My child support goes to guns
Once you've raised my cis-hetero
white seed
He will inherit my investment
Bleed for me overseas
In my name
The land of me
Land of the free
White oppressor
Withholder of reparation, salvation,
accreditation, justice, fairness,
independence

Don't worry
You can count on me
Mr. Enforcer
News reporter
Tally my body count
Return on investment
I know what's best
Death and taxes

And when it's all said and dead
I'll make a dollar off your leftover
debt

You shall not pass
Without my consent
Do not collect $200
Now go and consume
Cuz the only black that I like
Is the day after you thank me for
invading this country
Buying gifts for others
To celebrate my birthday

I am Him
Of Muslim descent
But I washed that sand off my skin
Even Saint Nick's beard is white
Snow
Sugar
Light at the end of the tunnel
All that is right
Is all that is _____

Laundry Day
01202016

I can't leave the wife and kids at home
For fear that we're living in a ghetto war zone
So we saddle up the tots
Grab the purse for my wife
Bundle up tight for a cold and snowy night

Halfway down the block
Come to forget the baby's bottle and pop
Trudge back home
Grab the milk and go again
Barely make the bus at a quarter past 10
Two babies
Two backpacks
Two twin duffle bags full of clothes
Four crumpled bills and change from my left pocket for our fare down the road

Full house on the bus on a Friday night
Everyone's dressed to the nines in their freshly pressed clothes
Staring at a lady in a red dress
In tall black stilettos
And a man in a vest
I get smacked in the head
Eyes stuck on the lady wrapped-up tight in red

My girl's yelling at me, jealous
I admit I was staring
Fantasizing about the day I could walk my wife into a shop and buy her the same

While the couples file off on the Broadway cross street
I'm stuck staring at the worn Jordans tied loose on my feet
The doors hiss closed as I hang my head down and yawn
The baby starts to cry when the milk's dried-up and gone

Kicked
03042016

Every time
I try to kick you
You kick right back

Habit
Rabbit
Dragon
Draggin' me
Down, down, down

Don't get no mercy
I'm on the ground
Dig in your heels
I'm reaching
Out, out, out

Grab hold
The end of my rope
And you cut

Slip through my fingers
Once again
I'm on my way
Down, down, down

Weapons of Mass Creation
04222016

Seed bombs and fungal mushroom clouds
Massive corporate undertakers
Government-subsidized farmers markets
Sustainability propaganda
Executive ordered lawn gardens
Wild no-fly zones
Global terra reform
Endangered house pet adoption
Red tidal waves
Birth rate regulation
Globally positioned excess food drops
Orbital solar plants
Petroleum prohibition and reclamation
Landfill infiltration
National Guardeners
Federal Seed Reserve
NASDAQ seed exchange
NOAA Naval Fleet

Sunrises
06032016

2/29 Parfait of clouds
3/1 Glass-blown marble wrapt in silk with cauliflower patterning
3/2 A pearl thrown in hand from the ocean
3/3 An angel's wing and a demon's arm floating in a river of blood /or/ A stack
of folded linens in the corner of a bed in a seaside cottage
3/4 Heartbeat in utero
3/7 Curtain call for an operatic interpretation of Reckoner by Radiohead
3/8 Lavender fabric softener floating in water
3/9 Superiority complex spotted in the distant past
3/14 Prayer flags casting threads to the wind
3/15 Soul growl of a dragon beneath a lake
3/16 The underside of a barrel rolling over a coral reef
3/17 The smoke from a flashbulb rising over a scene of the first picture ever taken
3/21 Looking at your problems with a hot towel over your face
3/22 Gyarados in repose
3/25 Belated berry pie
4/5 A wish made on an eyelash
4/6 A swathe of svelte silk sinking into a sea of fuchsian serenity
4/7 A hair of wisdom caught on a golden crown
4/8 The aftershock of an earthquake of love
4/12 Latte froth dripping on the floor as it's delivered
4/14 Blue (da ba dee da ba die)
4/15 A silver laser shot through the pink ether from the dark side of the moon,
propelling a sail to Alpha Centauri
4/16 Denver's Halo
4/19 Thanksgiving nap in the corner of the couch
4/20 Dante raising his brow at the spire of Paradiso
4/21 First gray hair on a youthful head
4/22 Seashell washed ashore and pulverized to pave a driveway
4/24 A mountain range of trees saying hello, gently blowing together to create a
maelstrom
4/26 |52| Mountains over Mountains; 4th changing line
4/27 Bright
4/28 Dryer sheet
5/2 Disappointing
5/3 Blister in the sun
5/5 The last missile ever launched on earth
5/6 Dry brush and drip
5/9 Cloud muscle
5/11 Putrid: A pile of rotting opossums
5/12 The yawning of Helios /or/ A pale of summer rainwater
5/13 A waif of Spring
5/16 Wood tip, wine, and smoke
5/27 Orca in storm-tossed waters
5/30 Titanic setting out across an uncharted iris
5/31 Helicopter chopping down the last bit of sky
6/2 Leftover dry erase marks
6/3 A splotched spray of indifference, indecision, and misdirection

142

"Hello, My Name Is"…ah, yes…the service year of 2015 to 2016. A time of departure from the familiar. "To the mountains!" I said, "Hello, Colorado. My name is Constantine. I am 24. Florida…well, I'd say it was nice, but I've had my fill of a near-quarter-century of your hot, wet, flat land and drug-fueled, surreal headlines."

I continued the trend of writing short stories and flash fiction here, some of which bled into writing poetry that tells more of a story than a simple gathering of observations or that plays with words. I discovered the I Ching (The Book of Changes, ancient Chinese oracle). I learned the detriment of the word "should." I made my first tag, "SKOO." I continued smoking Black & Milds. Weed is legal here! (And I don't care because it sends my brain into overdrive and my body *cannot* sit still or stop stretching.)

I was in Denver, CO for my AmeriCorps service year with City Year. I worked in a fifth-grade English classroom with a partner teacher. I spent this time wrestling with regret about my choice to break up with my last girlfriend, combined with departing my home state, family, and friends for the first time. I also could not, for the life of me, get a date, despite being on four dating apps. My landing in Denver was less than smooth but still exciting in some ways. I used Couchsurfing to coast from place to place for the first couple of months and rented a room for one or two months before I found a spot for the rest of the year. I managed to make friends with one host. We drank an inordinate amount of tea, and so began my initiation into tea drinking (cheers bud). I didn't live with any other corps members and most of them didn't get the best impression of me coming in. I was overeager and didn't have the same complaints about the program's expectations (always do your research, folks!). It didn't help that my partner teacher was less than stoked on the program and, by consequence, my presence in the classroom (this sometimes happens; it's a hand-you're-dealt kind of thing). I was basically shoved to the side until the final quarter of the year, then worked my ass off to make up all the tens of thousands of minutes I needed with my ten "focus group" students and ended-up with a couple thousand to spare.

So, this was a pretty isolated time for me. I was also carrying and projecting feelings of rejection from community criticism and controversy over my thesis in college. I was searching for my place in the world and wondering, "Why the fuck doesn't anybody like me? All I get is a handful of friends, and to everybody else I'm just an asshole?" Later in the year, more people got to know me and sought out more connection with me. At the same time, everyone was having an existential crisis by nature of the program: a gap year/service year either before or after college when we were all trying to figure out how to take the next step in life. Either way, I took things personally, sunk back into "lone wolf" mode, put my head down, and bulldozed through the year to make my commitment. I also got a job helping a guy to flip houses on the weekends between my 50-hour "work weeks" of volunteer service.

My birthday that year was *trash*. I turned 24. I had regular nightmares about my ex. I was in a new place, feeling alone and absolutely miserable.

Side story time! Visiting home for the holidays, I went on a wild trip to New Orleans for New Years for four days with a bunch of people I didn't know. We drove a barely operable electrician's van that was a pet project of one of the crew. We spray-painted a giant fleur des lis on the side. One headlight mostly worked in the dark, pouring rain on the highway. We had to jiggle the steering wheel the whole time to keep the wheels straight. We furnished the inside with a discarded bench seat, fake patio grass, blankets, and a cooler of unmentionables. Really, none of us knew each other save a weak connection to one out of the five people and a dog. We each had individual missions: busk for money, strip at as many places as possible for money/do all the drugs, steal a lawn flamingo, stay drunk the entire time, and play trombone with a big band. You can probably guess which one I was…that's right, stripping for money. Yes, we all accomplished our missions. Now, back to our regularly scheduled programming

The upside of City Year was the incredible amount of personal and professional development they invested in their corps on social justice, the education system, emphasis on self-care, and networking with a variety of fields to provide us with options to think about. This brought me to an earth-shattering realization in my career path. I had gone to therapy for the first time in college (it was free, I was writing the biggest paper of my life and designing a research study from scratch, debating my relationship, feeling a lot of social rejection, and it was *kind of* like free therapist training), after which I found myself thinking, "Man, therapy is pretty cool, but we should really do it outside. Maybe I can create that." Then, there it was. A recruiter from Outward Bound came for one of our monthly trainings and dropped those two little words in the same sentence: wilderness therapy. My gears starting whirring. He sent out an email later in the year about an Instructor Development Course with Colorado Outward Bound School (COBS) saying that we could use our Segal Education Award to pay for the course, and we could apply for an additional scholarship to cover the entire cost of the program.

Guess what I did? Good guess: I ignored it and went back home to live with my mother. Ha! No, not really…well, kind of (more on that later). I used my Education Award, got a supplemental scholarship from COBS, and spent all my saved weekend house-flipping money on gear for the trip. As luck would have it, the guy at the gear consignment shop had been a COBS instructor for 11 years, so he knew exactly what I needed. Thanks, universe. In the end, I did manage to come out with a few friends from the Corps and my tea buddy from Couch-surfing. In the intimacy department, I had almost no women in my life, and my heart started to scab over again. That said, I was on the cusp of a prospective come-to-Jesus moment.

Thunder dies
A cloud hangs over

Descend into silence
Be smart with your heart

You are the wind
I am the sail//

Volume

////VIII////

Contribute

07012016 // 11242016

Ages 24 - 25

76% Water
07012016

Sit & listen
There, you hear
Drown out the inside
Turn you inside out
Look at your heart

Life, a pulse of spring
Dead of winter in between

A drop ripples in a puddle
Overflows
Trickles into streams
Down into falls of white water

How many times have you been reminded?
Not only by screaming waterfalls
By snow-crunching whispers
Land-carving repetition

Have you not believed them until now?
Awe quietly creeps in
Headwaters drip
In dark and light
In fight or flight
Whence dust shall return
We are 76% water

Soapy
07132016

Sometimes, you find a pocket of the world that seems like it was made just for you. Maybe you actually were the first one to pee on that tree, to breathe in its beauty, to appreciate the way the light burrows into the scenery, to enjoy a meal there, alone. Chances are, someone else has had the exact same thought at that exact same spot.

There are 7 billion people on earth and that number is rising. There's just as many ants in a few dozen super-colonies. More than 600 identified species have gone extinct by our hand, or extension thereof. Trees crowd together by the millions per forest to protect themselves and plankton shuffle past each other in panic by the boiling ocean parts per million.

Beyond the dust of a window ledge, our planet swings in a vacuum, affectionately attached to its warm, loving everything: the sun. That celestial elemental rules over our ability to live with gravitas and many have looked on in worship.

Inside that dust mote floating in a slice of sun peering over the window-sill, there are just as unfathomable a collection of atoms, and our Celestine life-giver could easily be estranged and forgotten from our galactic structure without notice.

The stars of our galaxy are salt grains in an ocean, fluttered upon by planktonic wafts. Yet, our galactic slurry is still just a spill on the sidewalk of our Texas-sized local intergalactic cluster, which you have to squint to see revolving around the true center of all that is and ever will be for us in this existence.

And this

This is it

This is everything.

All that we can ever possibly concern ourselves with from beginning to end, from light to dark, from endless surface area to radiating core.

This is our bubble.

And our bubble is a thin, short-lived whim of air floating over an ocean of eternity, surviving only as long as it can avoid colliding with the other clouds of bubbles or spontaneously popping from instability.

Just one soft breath, held aloft for an instant, like so many others, beautifully undulating and swirling with soapy colors.

A child admires the many bubbles they blow. One pops. They dunk their wand in the soap again, happy to blow hundreds more.

Chances are, someone else has had the exact same thought at that exact same spot; but then, there is a chance that person was you.

147

Succubus
07202016

Teach me all your venomous lessons
Humble me with your mammoth repose
Sweeten my senses with floods of sensation
Grapple my attention with wind-shaken boughs
Hurl my affections across the expanse
Drain me dry of any notion of self

Absorb every inkling that permeates my brain
And rain them refiltered upon my flesh
Drink of my blood, though I swat you indignant
Circle and buzz when my focus wavers
Burn my being even as I seek refuge
Freeze my fingers, lest they lust for anything else
I char your remains just to stare in amazement
I drink of your fluids to replenish my own
I gnaw at your fruit to fill the void in my center

You surround me
You coat me in your filth and I bask
You whisper in gurgles
You whine in small drones
You scream in loud claps and my ear nearly explodes
Blinded and deafened
Blistered, burned and bruised
Scraped, scratched, frozen and used
My demise goes unnoticed
You refuse me on reflex
Another will come to witness you

White Rafters
08062016

Sweat in my eyes
Poltergeist
Blood spilled in the coffin

So far from the light
I can barely see you
Don't turn your head
Lay down and die

The end is nigh
Open my skull
Just for you
It's what you do to me

It's the power of your rhetoric
In this existence
Lay down and die

Jaded
08102016

Jaded

It's the meaning of the word
Every ounce of happiness I have
Weighed down by some hurt

The amnesia that I get
Forget all the good I've felt
The moment's sadness drips into
That dark and depthless well

It's the cross that I bear
A cloak that shields me from myself
Just a tinge
A subtle hue

Jaded

A Fool's Errand
08102016

At last, across 2,000 miles
Extending for a touch
Kicking through dead leaves and
snow
Nothing ventured
Nothing gained

I caught a fire
From a spark
Lying dormant
In my heart

I felt it's old familiar warmth
But breathed into it warily
Cautiously fanned the flames
Within my chest

Time soon built up my resolve
Tearing down my mortar walls
Eastern winds blew in and fed them
My hunger grew for fruits afar

Landscapes rose and fell behind
Winds swept clouds across the sky
No mind nor time, in front of me
Burned the apple of my eye

A cold and silent winter's night
I found the orchard by torch light
Dormant trees awaiting springs
release
Bare and cloaked in white

Yet one red Apple hung for me
Suspended in time by winter's cold
I gave pause to admire
To honor the distance I had come

Across 2,000 miles
Slowly reaching for what I so
longed
My hand shook from excitement
and the cold

Reflecting in my eye
My fingers neared their first
embrace

So intent on my indulgence
I could not notice my mistake

The only light by which I saw
My torch which gave me strength
Just as weary from our travels
Had a hunger all its own

Embers dribbled from its flames
And licked the branches as it
glowed
As I touched the fruit, it bit the bark
Engorging, lighting bright the dark

I caught a fire from a spark
Carried a torch across the land
But grasped the fruit with burning
hands

The dormant orchard, engulfed in
flame
Set its embers to my skin
I fled the apple I desired
Betrayed by my fiery old friend

Reflections on Outward Bound
08292016

It's two-past-lunch and we're in the middle of the Mojave Desert. You may be thinking the Mojave Desert is a bit off-course from the Rockies to Alaska, that's because we've already finished and we're currently en route to the annual national Wilderness Therapy Symposium in Park City, Utah. I say "we"; I'm referring to my friend and me, a friend I made on-course with Outward Bound.

At course start, there were 22 of us, split into two patrols, but not everyone made it. Some only made day two (I was nearly one of them), some made week two, or a few more weeks. By course-end on day fifty-two, there were 15 left standing by the Alaskan Pacific, or sitting, or hobbling (me). For Raphael and I, we consider ourselves on day sixty-four. We plan on taking our experience straight to the field to grab us a couple of jobs at the Symposium in Utah and we figured it was an opportune time to do a little extra soul-searching and bonding aided by the conventions of modern machinery in a cross-country road trip. We've crashed at a different house nearly every night since we left Alaska and everyone we meet is astounded to hear that we've only known each other these two months, expecting to hear at least ten years.

Outward Bound is an experience like none other in so many ways, choosing which ways to express that can be difficult. For me, it's Raphael. On day one something just clicked, and we had no idea what was in store for us. We, like most people who embark on an Outward Bound trip, were in search of something greater. Life began to collect dust, to reflect itself. There was not much to look forward to, or at least there wasn't much looking forward. On course, you're forced to pick your head up and look around you; if you don't, you're bound to get lost. So, there we were, Patrol A (A.K.A. The Rambling Butt Pikas), lost and trying to find our way out of our old, familiar harbors and into the exciting unknown.

The first three days were possibly the most difficult for us because we had so much to adapt to and so much inertia to shake off. Day zero was an assemblage of all course attendees and a gear issuing. We met our patrols and leaders, got the layout for the next couple months, and planted the seeds for relationships to grow. On the second day, I slid down a snow pass and injured my knee as I turned to face the mountain and catch myself. We had a patrol member who agreed to leave the course because her allergies, asthma, and anxiety would not permit her to keep pace. We both hiked out the next day, and I was unsure how badly I injured my knee. We spent the night at basecamp in Leadville, Colorado talking about the incredible journey we'd been on so far in such a short time. I was relieved to find out my MCL was sprained, not torn, and with a sturdy knee brace and a heaping regiment of ibuprofen, I could continue so long as I felt capable.

Our patrol was reunited on day six for resupply and I enjoyed helping put things together and seeing how things operate behind the scenes up until that point. Raphael and I were up most of the night catching up on the days I missed, searching for constellations, and swapping life stories. We left the next morning for what would be one of the best campsites we stayed at. Centered on a heaping boulder slab, horseshoed by mountain tops, with an open view of more mountain chains in the distance, we spent four days and three nights there. We enjoyed baths in a freezing creek nearby running-off from snowmelt. We designed mock lesson plans and practiced teaching each other. We worked through snow school, learning how to properly step-climb in snow, self-arrest with an ice ax, how to fall and how to communicate commands. We earned our first day of freedom. As our instructors scouted a fitting place for a peak attempt, we navigated ourselves back to camp, cooked, and fulfilled our daily duties before relaxing and waiting for them to return. The following day, we awoke with stars still bright in the sky at three in the morning. Once our instructors led the climb, we followed in sets of three until everyone was halfway up. Unfortunately, the peak ended-up being impassable and our first peak attempt stayed just that, an attempt, but we all still had a great time.

The end of our mountaineering section in the Gore Range was one of my favorite days. I was the navigator for the day and we were faced with an impossibly steep slope to get down. I took lead and made all the decisions for micro-navigating each step so each of us would be safe. It was a great opportunity to practice setting pace, communication, navigation, and to face any fear I accumulated from my first steep slope spill. It took us nearly three hours to descend only one thousand feet, but it was well-timed because it began to rain just as we reached the bottom. The truck was waiting for us at the trailhead the next day and while we were excited for the snacks and showers to come, we were baffled at how we could drive an hour and cover the same distance it just took us two weeks to hike. We engorged ourselves with snacks at the local supermarket, devoured Mike's delicious cooking at basecamp, and slept like rocks in our dormitory beds. Of course, being reunited again with the other patrol, we only slept after hours of catching-up.

Up next was our rock-climbing section in Vedauwoo, Wyoming. We all took full advantage of our six-hour road trip at every stop, loading up on common snacks which would soon be delicacies to us again. At camp, we were split into four climbing groups, and Raphael and I agreed to split so we could get to know some other folks better (we thoroughly enjoyed each other's company). I learned how to set anchors around trees and rocks, how to use artificial gear, so long as there's three points of solid contact. I learned commands for belaying, how to coil rope, clip through transfer points, conduct safety checks, and crack climb (that's climbing by jamming parts of your body into a tight crack). On the fourth of July, I taught my second lesson - a more fully developed one than our initial practice runs in the Gore Range - about building and caring for campfires. It went well and every campfire to come was accompanied by someone commenting on which log structure was being used, keeping water nearby, clearing the area and making sure the fire was out at night's end. At night, Raphael and I stayed with our third tent mate, Ryan, and would for the rest of the course. We spent most nights playing our favorite two made-up card games and making fun of each other. We divided up into teams at the end of our time in Vedauwoo to teach kids about rock climbing to put our skills to the test and again back at base in Leadville and it went brilliantly! Another week down, we packed camp and saddled-up back to Leadville for the Wilderness First Responder course.

Having just camped for another week and made it half-way through course, our body odors warranted another round of showers and our spirits needed a town day. After a long and complicated procession of who showered after whom, our first stop in town was the laundromat to get a deep-clean after weeks of soil embedded in our gear.

We spent several days absorbing a litany of information, did some bloodletting, and had a massive, fully orchestrated wilderness emergency scenario: a plane crash. We were split into teams of three or four and assigned responder roles within our factions. I was the leader of mine. We responded as best we could, given our short time to master the skills taught to us and we performed passably but not exceptionally. I became a certified Wilderness First Responder! To finish our time at base in Leadville, we did a base beautification service project. We also examined maps, planned routes, food rations, gear lists and projected mileage with a rate of travel to prep for our practical.

The final leg of our journey was at hand, but first, a 3-day solo for us to reflect on everything we'd accomplished so far and set intentions for the final test: Alaska. We had two weeks to practically apply our skills as our instructors shadowed us from several hundred yards behind. We flew out of Denver, transferred in Seattle, and landed in Anchorage. The shuttle from the airport down the Kenai Peninsula was absolutely mind-melting. We were riding along black sand beaches, looking across the bay to lush mountains jutting up from the beach shrouded in clouds within 1,000 feet of sea level. My mouth hung open for hours.

Our two patrols were divided mostly according to age and set out on opposite journeys. Our group would start by climbing the Exit Glacier up to the Harding Ice Field for a week of snow camping. We learned about rigging a team to traverse a glacier safely: a maximum team of 4 tied approximately 30 feet away from each other and reading the terrain so we cross perpendicular to any possible crevasses. The team anchor holds the compass and uses the team in front of them as the line of travel. We had to stay in-sync with each other step-for-step so the rope between each person barely kissed the ice. This is in case someone falls into a crevasse, the others can self-arrest with their ice axes and the rope will not be so taught as to immediately pull the whole team in and not so loose that the person falling snaps their neck when they reach the end of the rope's stretch.

We alternated with the other patrol to complete our journey with a week of bushwhacking in the Alaskan backcountry in the Chugach Range, rotating leadership and chores roles each day while operating completely self-sufficient from our instructors who trailed behind. I led a summit up a mountain in a hailstorm. There were several moments when different people wanted to call it, but I managed to convince and rally us up to the top and we were all hypothermic by the time we got there. The capstone of everything was a 5-mile run to the beach (I jogged, walked, then hobbled) where we circled-up and had the opportunity to explain why we earned our Outward Bound pins (a badge of honor for completing a rigorous course). Each of us stated our case and when it came to me, I declined my pin because I felt I was not yet truly "outward bound". I was still yet to leave the safety of my harbor. Enduring hardship in the outdoors is something I'm long-familiar with through my days in scouting. The true challenge, for me, is launching from everything I know at home and establishing myself as a guide with a wilderness therapy company.

Self-Talk
09222016

      You have no job. You have no plan. Your toenails are painted two different shades of blue. You have no car. You're watching bootleg cartoons online. You're afraid to do anything. You're prolonging making any real-life commitments or responsibilities on a 1-2 month road trip across the country. You have idiotic stick figure tattoos on your feet. You have no girlfriend and you can't even get a date or a girl that's interested in you. Your mom pays for your phone bill. You have no place else to go. You've been living out of a suitcase for the past year+. You collect porn. You've only ever had 4 girlfriends, the longest of which was 1 year, and even that had a 2-week hiatus slapped in the middle of it. You don't have any mentionable skills. You keep a diary. Your knee is fucked up. You are a loser. You are a pussy. Get your shit together.

      12:00 PM

      You're looking for jobs after you went on a 2-month instructor development course across the Rocky Mountains and Alaska - which you didn't have to pay a dime for, thanks to grants and scholarships. You dove into a field to see if you would like it. You're reconsidering and you injured your knee. You have touched all 4 corners of this country in one summer, made a new lifelong friend, united old ones, had your fantasy cross-country graduation trip and did all of it in the ballpark of $2,000-2,500. For your 25th (and golden) birthday, you were networking at a symposium in Park City, Utah, still sweating from bombing down a mountain on your first mountain bike ride. You went to your dream college, did a service year with AmeriCorps, continue to intentionally build your résumé, and you settle for nothing less than amazing at almost everything. You do what's right and stand up for yourself and others. You have the best friends and family anyone could ask for. You can survive (even thrive) with only a suitcase-worth of clothes and belongings. Your porn collection is top-notch and diverse. You gave back so that you can do what you're doing right now. It's no secret that everyone you meet wants to be doing what you're doing. You don't make excuses. You're no worse-off. Keep it up.

      Love, C.
      12:32 PM

Homegrown Love
10032016

Layin nekit on the bet afta frech chowa. Everyone's wondering how long I'm staying for. My friends and family want me around. It's nice to see them again. I don't enjoy not having a car to travel autonomously, to make it easier to hang out with people, to do anything really. I don't enjoy "staying" with my mother, on her dollar, without knowing for how long, without a job, or a place of my own to come back to. At that point, it's not a visit, it's a staycation. I'm temporarily living here. It's embarrassing. It's crippling. It's a story drawn-out too long, revisiting the same circumstances too often. My own income, my own space, my own vehicle, my independence to feel empowered - these are the things I want, and they will come once I commit to them. For now, I haven't seen anyone in nine months, and I've been making my rounds, trying to relax and enjoy, not to think about what I want, trying to cherish what I do have. It's good to be around homegrown love. It's good to be supported. It's good not to be rushed. It's good to be making this journey to add to my story. It's good to be heard. It's good to have options and opportunities to look forward to. Life is good. Cherish what you got.

Dear R
11242016

  What a pleasant surprise your letter was, and what a beautiful surprise you are in my life. Thousands of miles, weeks and months on my feet, on the road, our paths intersected over drums and sweat. Two years after our surface interactions reached unknown depths in just two days. Almost two months later, who could have guessed? We're sending each other letters.

  You've been a blessing in my life. I look forward to seeing your texts waiting for me. I appreciate your well-wishes for my jobs. It feels good to be working again. The next step is a car. After that, a career. These days are full of stress, but you give me something to look forward to.

  You're doing everything right in college. Roommates, friends, homework, thesis, self-care. You're really invested in developing yourself and your education, and that's admirable.

  You're amazing. Don't ever stop.

  Luv,
  Constantine

Reflections on Volume VIII

"Contribute" happens fast—all within 2016 as a 25 year-old—and picks up at a milestone: I graduated City Year the same time my close friend graduated college, who was a year behind me. We met up with another friend from New College for a graduation trip canoeing the St. Regis Loop in the Adirondack Mountains and called ourselves the "St. Regis Sirens," not that anyone was around to hear.

Enough of that, back to Denver, to Leadville for COBS, and the beginning of an exciting career in wilderness therapy! Two days into a 52-day course, I slipped on a snow-covered mountainside and tweaked my left knee. Great. Urgent Care told me to quit. Not an option, I was all in at that point. I was going to become a field guide or break my leg trying (that's good luck, right?). I went back on course all bionic and medicated.

I started to feel the effects of being in nature for weeks on end. I felt...*good*...peaceful, accepting, happy, grounded, purposeful. I was pursuing a dream. I actually had a dream! Yes! I could feel the plaque of sadness breaking down, replaced with the free-flowing blood of passion! I finished the course with a new friend. We went on a cross-country road trip. We had the time, money, and it was on our bucket lists.

We started in Denver, to Boulder, to the Wilderness Therapy Symposium in Utah. This birthday was excellent! I turned 25 (Golden Birthday! August 25th). I mountain biked for the first time with my friend, reminding myself to breathe and failing to keep my knuckles from turning white, showed up to a networking session covered in dirt and sweat in a bandana, and started chatting up wilderness programs. We cleared the Mojave Desert at 120 mph to Los Angeles (speeding ticket in hand), where my friend promptly relapsed into drug use and shit all over his brother's girlfriend's white, leather couch in Beverly Hills...On to the redwoods! To the Sequoias! Through the Mojave again to the Grand Canyon (we walked through a prescribed burn outside the park. Epic!), the Petrified Forest, Austin, Houston, to New Orleans. In Florida, we visited my dad (he'd returned stateside because Greece's economy collapsed three times and he couldn't find a job) and New College friends. We parted ways at my home in St. Petersburg. We lost touch due to disagreements over his drug use and my way of addressing it.

I was stuck at home with my mother for an indefinite period of time because I had no insurance and, as a result, no idea what the story was with my knee. I might have blown my only chance at having a dream by simply trying to pursue it. Once again, I felt hopeless. I got a graveyard job merchandising with Home Depot and a front desk job at a gym during the day. I slept, meal prepped, and shopped for a car in the four to six hours between shifts, with one day off a week. I was grinding my way back to my independence. Although, it was nice to reconnect with family and friends after my first significant stint away. I also connected with a girl at New College and invested more of myself than I should have, but I welcomed the ego boost.

Through this darkness, I accrued nuggets and lessons about loving myself, doing things for my own sake, the therapy of being outside, etc. Those tools came in handy when battling the anxiety and depression about whether I still had a shot at my dream career in wilderness therapy. Then, Trump got elected president...what a cherry on top.

Broken mirror
Ancient pottery
Abandoned cinema
Dormant tree
Tarnished penny

Tell me
What new beauty and utility does time bestow?//

Volume /////IX/////

Life

is a Sketch

12102016 // 12042017

Ages 25 - 26

55 Hours in 4 Days
12102016

Finally getting some paychecks. Got some test drives to do. Looking at Honda CR-V or Toyota RAV4 around $12-15k. Feeling much better now that I'm working. I expect to feel even better with my own transportation and making monthly payments on my own. I need a new laptop, too. I can buy refurbished, monthly payments on new, or save and buy outright. My wardrobe is maturing too. These little steps, small successes, inches of progress, make me feel better. They are material, but they represent growth, maturity, independence, professionalism. I can see these changes in me; my views and values. I'm gaining experience to inform who I am, who I want to be, and what I value.

You cannot have a fully informed opinion about life until you have lived on your own.
04:18 AM

Night Walk
12182016

Couldn't sleep. Had to go for a night walk for a self-pep-talk. The following is a tribute to said talk:

3 months, man. 3 months. You've been here for 3 months and look at what you've accomplished. You've landed two great jobs with bosses who care about you and want to help you out. I know you're feeling down from time to time about staying with your mom—feeling like a mommy's boy, a pussy, a bitch, emasculated and immature—but you have to know that is not the case. 3 months! You came home after a grand adventure, a dream adventure of a lifetime! You touched all. Four. Corners. Of the country. In a single summer! The Adirondacks. Alaska. Los Angeles. Ft. Lauderdale. You saw all your friends and family. You came home and it was not for lack of a plan. You had a plan! A great one! But like you always say, "Sometimes you have plans for life and sometimes life has plans for you." You got injured, but even then, that didn't stop you! You went into that Outward Bound Instructor Development Course to have fun, to reward yourself for all your hard work in City Year, to build your resume, and to investigate, immerse yourself, and pursue a career path you were deeply interested in. You had a big dream of starting your own wilderness therapy organization (which can still happen!) and you went for it! 100% would have been calling it off at the injury and returning after you recovered, 105% would have been pushing through the course despite your knee injury, but you went 110% and still followed through with the wilderness therapy symposium and networked and mountain biked for the first time twice on your 25th birthday (with a new best friend)!

Now, your knee still hurts and you're working a week and a half's worth of hours in half a week! 3 months! You came home, got through your depression, got two jobs, got a great girl in your life that you drive down once a month or more to see all weekend, fine-tuned your resumé, cover letters, trained for two jobs, sifted through nearly 1,000 cars online, in-person, test drove, nearly signed-off on one (but listened to your gut and the universe and made the right decision for you), are helping your mom, and you got to apply your WFR in real life by slinging your mom's arm when she fell and shattered her shoulder! It's a lot. You've learned so much in such a short time. Done so much. Seen so much! You're a great guy! They look at you and they say, "Man, what an awesome guy. I wanna be that guy. I want to help that guy. I want to be around that guy. I want to hang out with that guy. (I want to fuck that guy!)" That's what they say. You're awesome. Please don't see yourself as a "pussy".

Know that you really are great. The money will come, the car will come, the career will come, your place will come. You refuse to settle for anything less than perfect on your own terms, and people admire that and respect that. You're fine. You're doing fine. You're doing better than fine, you're doing GREAT! Keep busting your ass. You. Are. Not. Lazy. You are not entitled like so many other people. You earn what you get and you earn it with respect. Really, you're doing great. I know it's a lot and I know it's overwhelming but at the end of the day (or night, or beginning of the day, or whenever you get off work now) when you crash or take it easy for a bit you know you've *earned* it and that's the best feeling of all!

You've made so many of your dreams come true already, and when you find that perfect car that you've been waiting for for years, you'll know that *you* did it for *you*. You make your dreams come true! You're dedicated, and you're blowing peoples' minds with your dedication and yours should be blown too! 3 months, man. It will come in time, at the right time, on your time. I know it seems like forever ago already but the past few years have been packed with growth, accomplishment, and achievement for you. You touched all four corners of the country in one summer, you went on a month-long, 7,000-mile road trip, you completed a hardcore 2-month backcountry hike, you gave back in service to the future generation of our country, you completed a thesis in–literally–record time at New College, you powered through your Associate's at SPC, you toured the Mediterranean alone with a rolling carry-on, you reconnected with your father, you met your sister, you fell in love multiple times in different ways and *you* finished them when they went against your gut, you got off your ass and started making something of yourself after partying your insides out, *you* motivated *so* many people to do and make better of themselves! You're crushing it! You will find your place in time and you've done everything right for yourself to build the best-possible future for future you. You truly are a "great man". Good people doing good things for good reasons, and you're one of them among the many others you keep around you. Today, you're going car shopping with your mother in Sarasota and Bradenton, another step toward your dream car and your dream independence. For now, flourish and enjoy that interdependence of doing it amongst family and friends because it's all a blessing and it can go by in a flash.

You are truly is beautiful.
06:58 AM

Graveyard
02022017

It's getting harder to tell when today ends and yesterday begins so
I nap in between
It's getting harder to stand up straight so
I go to the gym

I can drive between sunrise and sunset with this smile on my face
I can swipe, like, and subscribe on my break
They say you're more emotionally susceptible when you're exhausted
They say exhaustion makes you more emotionally susceptible

Sometimes my eyes close at red lights
Short naps
Crash into
Sleep Sessions
Micro Naps
Sleeping in between blinks

There's only so many places to go in the middle of the night if you're alone
There's only so many kinds of people that are out at that time of night if they're
not home
My thoughts ride pogo sticks

Asleep at the Wheel
02172017

It's Monday
But I haven't slept for 23 hours straight
Already setting-up my third shift
Sun's coming up
Night's going down
I got a limp
I hope tomorrow I can lay down
Skip shower
Too tired to brush my teeth
Food still stuck
My stomach's growl
But eyes making friends with gravity

At this point
I want a girl to come and some warm tea home
I made love to a last
Nice to sit chair and relax just minute
God...
Damnit...

Budget
02172017

$210 car payment
$140 car insurance
$75 gas
$80 student loans
$450 food
$150 credit card
$200 fun

$1350 monthly expenses
$1750 income
Save $400/mo

$20,000 line of credit
$3,000 used
$17,000 / 85% available

$14,000 auto loan
$16,000 student loans
$30,000 total debt

A Future Self
02232017

Ear gauged with buffalo horn dragon
Cassiopeia covered with color constellation scene
Autoger super-sized
Feet tats removed/covered
Plays trombone, drums, guitar, harmonica, and sings in a blues band
Has MSW and LPSW in psychology
Has a successful motivational blog
Tours with a band half the year
Tours as a motivational speaker the other half
Fully diversified/invested for retirement
Gives 15% of income to charities
Participates in dozens of demonstrations and petitions for rights each year
Vertical gardening hobby
Lives in a large, totally open floor plan apartment
Owns leading wilderness therapy organization revolutionizing and popularizing the industry, operated by trusted colleagues
Certified carpenter, plumber, welder, and mechanic
Licensed masseuse
Francesca RAV4
Harley Sportster bike, flat black/chrome
Has a dozen patents, open-sourced after 5 years of production
Has 2 pet sugar gliders and 2 morning doves
Created a federal holiday near tax return season dedicated to donating money to charities
Fluent in Spanish
Has built homes in Salamanca, New Orleans, Micronesia, Bali, Peru, and Largo
Involved in the international effort to develop artificial intelligence morality
Working to drastically lower the amount of sugar available in the American diet

Tree Rings
03122017

Another soon-to-be sleepless night
Tonight, I need to make good use of
these insomniatic hours
Slept all day
More beating myself up
More wasted time
More helpless whining without
action
I haven't even looked at jobs
I avoid it
I'm biding time, waiting for
everything to be done for me
Waiting for praise
To be told what to do
To have my mind made-up for me
To be gently pushed and suggested
into the next step on my path
Never thinking for myself
Never deciding for myself
Unsure at every moment, every turn

"Just tell me what to do," my
actions cry for help
"Leave me alone, I can do it
myself," my words betray
Why do I evade adult life?
Why do I yearn so for
independence while stifling that
same craving with defiant wait?
I'm driving myself to despair
I'm stigmatizing myself
I'm beating and beating and
beating, retreating, relinquishing
my right to myself to advance
I can't stand it
This time
This stagnancy
This uncertain future

I'm surrounded by belief and
support
The rest is my own to make
My own to decide
To act
To be brave
To move
To embrace the unknown and fall in
love with my own volition,

unhindered by excuses to continue
to be unhappy
This unhappiness will be my own
This dissatisfaction will weigh on
me alone to quell
A living wage
A space of my own
Free time to explore
New hobbies and interests to
discover
New friends to make
All the available resources to push
myself to be better, to be happier

It would be best to live without any
expectations
Reality = Happiness - Expectations
As they say
But how can I?
How can I shed expectations of
myself, of others, of the future, of
events and places and things?
To never be disappointed by
anyone or anything, including
myself?
To truly be free?
I want too much, and therein lies
the problem
Lying about expectations
For without expectations there is no
motivation for growth and if in
growth is my happiness...
Like a tree, I will grow until dead
and know contentment

SPACE SPACE, inc.
04062017

Abandoned warehouse
Trailer to live on property
Solar/Wind power
Collect rain water
Square Acct/reader to swipe on
iPad
Feminine hygiene products in
bathroom
Guest book
Free Table
$1 bin
Science Weekly/Nat Geo/DuPont
subscriptions
Security system
Fish tanks (connected to hydro
garden)
Scrap metal statues
Pyramid
Fruit trees
Post in Westword, Pearl St Flyers,
Meetup, Facebook, Birdy
Couchsurfing
Quiet room
Free earplugs
Bee farm

Day time (sales)
Succulents
Records/ free local zines
Coffee
Tea
Books
Classic games
Comics
Holistic hygiene
Rocks/gems/wrapped jewelry
Used camping gear
Fetish gear? 18+?
Chips/candy/drinks/Ashley's baked
goods
Vertical Garden with tables
Donation/thrift shop

Night time
Hookah
Venue
Kava/Kratom
Arcade

Sunday: Church of Controller
competitive gaming (d-pad cross
and button rays of light)
Monday: Drum Circles
Twosday: Indie Movie double
feature
Wednesday: Night Sky Tour
Thursday: Hookah
Friday/Saturday: Shows

Merch shop
Josh! Stuff
Ashley S's stuff
Josh D's stuff
Eli/Michelle's merch
Stans drums
Band merch inventory/logbook
Inkmonstr
Framed memes
Local gov't voting info

SPACE SPACE YouTube Channel
Interview artists with old A/V
equipment
Live graffiti painting
Live venue stream

Gallery/art exhibitions:
Graffiti space
History of Colorado/Denver exhibit

Classes:
Art
Yoga
Meditation

SPACE SPACE Community Fund
Homeless
Rehab
Planned parenthood
Suicide prevention
3rd World Water

Secure credit card
Social media/Product Shopper
2 Baristas
Street team

Life on Hold
04102017

Where do I see myself in 5 years?
Where do I see myself in 10 years?
What do I need to get there?
How can I get what I need?
When is the earliest I can get it?
Who will help me get it?
My future is my plan. Without a plan, I will be stuck exactly where I am now, doing what I am now. If I don't know where I'm going, I will go nowhere. If I act on a faulty or short-term plan, I am liable to fall back into the same pattern again, stuck surviving until I cook-up another faulty, short-term quick fix.

"There comes a time when we are all told we can no longer play the child's game, some at 18, some at 30, some at 40 years-old, but we are all told sooner or later."
- Moneyball

I am 25. I can no longer play the child's game. There is no more "try", I have to do. I need a plan. I must act. I have to take a risk. I have to make up my own mind and be my own man. I have to take responsibility because it's all on me now. It's my life. It's my decision. It's up to me to do it for myself, and it's long overdue. I can no longer put off the inevitable with childish dreams and wonder and ideas and reckless abandon. I am my own responsibility. The more I talk about it, the worse I feel, because it's more talking and less doing and the reality of it is still sitting there, waiting for me to face it when I put down this pen, and I close this book, and I get out of this car, and I go up to bed, and I go to sleep, and I wake up, and I do it all over again and again and again and again, and I build myself up, and I knock myself down, and I pity my own gutless immaturity – until when? Until when? When do I grow up? I wish I would have started sooner. I wish I would have been more prepared. I wish I had more time. I wish I could go back and make myself do then what I have to do now. I wish it was already over. I wish I was already there. I wish I knew how to. I wish I wasn't afraid. I wish I could be brave. I wish I didn't pity myself. I wish I didn't wish. I wish I knew what to do. I wish I knew what I want. I wish I could just do it. I wish it wasn't so hard. I wish it wasn't such a big deal. I wish I could enjoy the ride. I wish I could be more grateful for what I have. I wish I had more help. I wish I didn't have to do it alone. I wish I would have done it right from the beginning. I wish I didn't feel like such a fuck-up. I hope I can figure it out.

Clumsy Poem of Grief
04112017

Looking back now I can say
It's been a couple of years
But it seems only yesterday
Was the day I left you in tears

That tortured look on your face
I see it in my nightmares
Knowing the fault is mine
I'm the reason it's there

And now the time I spend each and every day
Replaying feelings, I'm feeling, you're feeling
Remembering how I was the villain to you

I know that at the time I was your superhero
Mr. Do-No-Wrong, Golden God from above
I couldn't shoulder the pressure for you
Couldn't come through and make it true

But baby you were worth every ounce of the weight
And I'm so sorry I kept you waiting
How you chased after me so sure of what you wanted

Didn't flaunt it, just tried to capture me
And all that time I swept you to the side
Because I had too much on my mind

I know it's a crime the way I treated you, didn't treat you
Nothing to do but regret what I put you through

God knows I tried to apologize
But it didn't come out right
Just turned into a fight
The guilt weighs so heavy on my conscience
I couldn't be conscious of my comments

I wish I could sing you to sleep
Make you smile and laugh instead of just weep
But I'm weak, I thought I could be strong for you
But what's a boy to do when he doesn't have a clue

But you do, and I ain't worried about your way in this world
You're the smartest girl I ever had the pleasure of loving
My hugs and kisses to your future
I'm wishing all the best to you

Depressive Stream of Consciousness
04132017

Struggle together. Suffer together. Smoke together. Stop together. Show up together. Slow together. This is not enough. No one will ever see. I will never know. This is not enough. Time is taken. Can't return. Time slows in agony. Accelerates in bliss. To feel everything in every moment. To experience all. To be able to savor. To appreciate. To feel the moment. To suffer. To miss it. For it to pass unannounced. Unaffected. Bliss is numbing. Succumbing to forfeiture of emotional range. Disengage. Dismantle everything inside. Without. Sitting. Waiting. Dive down. Consume. Clutch. Wait. This will not end. This moment will not pass. I cannot see beyond. I cannot release the past. I cannot confide in myself. I cannot. Accomplish. Anything. All my successes are failures. Always fallen short. Never enough. Never perfect. Never complete. Everything slides between my grasp. I will never achieve happiness. Unobtainable. Always turn towards the dark. Look away from the sun. This is who I am. Always be. Never evolve. Never transform. Nevermore. Cheapening past. Inflating future. Losing value. Meaningless exchange. Drift across nothing into void. Defy everything. Misstep. Fall. And fall. And fall. And fall. Never to stand again.

Tire Swing
04152017

First time I saw you
You were 4 inches tall
Laid out flat on a screen
I could touch you
Maybe you touched me

Even though we both had mutual interest
When we started speaking wasn't my decision
You made me smile and I even laughed
Gave me your number when I didn't even ask

I may have been skeptical
But I felt you were something special
Plans got knocked off the first time we tried
Thought you were running scared, I ain't gonna lie

Damn near had a heart attack when you replied
And agreed we could push it back
Even down to the minute we were meeting-up
Thought you were having second thoughts, ghosting, freezing-up

But it went so well I still couldn't believe
Two nights in a row, second date to three
Even offered to pay for me so I knew you weren't trying to get something for free

You were interested in more of me
So I drove us around town telling you my life story
Struggling, staying up late just to sit next to me

You even moved in on the first kiss
Awkwardly captured your lips
So excited that I almost missed
Fumbling just to come to grips
"Can shit really happen like this?"

So it just goes to show
You don't know and I don't know but I know that
I don't wanna say no to any opportunity to be with you
See this through, see what's true

Formula
06112017

      Laughter really is the best medicine. Humor is the number-one survival skill. That's in any survival situation, really; the wild, a relationship, day-to-day life. Sometimes I care about people who are complicated. Everything is simple. And I think I might be one of those complicated people. In reality, I just haven't figured out my simplicity. The universe was complicated. Light, space-time...then Einstein came along. $E=MC^2$. I'm not complicated, I just haven't figured out my formula. Some people do, and they're the happy ones. Chaos is complicated. Chaos is just order, misunderstood. Find the pattern. Find what makes it simple. Can you bring order to chaos?

      Solve for X: What do I want?

      When you get what you want...what you need...the rest just becomes extra, a bonus.

Dónde Palabras Me Han Fallado
08062017

Yo recuerdo cuando estuvimos júntos. Había dolores, pero había buenos tiempos también. Pienso en ti cada día. Te siento en el corazón. Yo tengo dolores y buenos tiempos allí así como. Te vi saliendo la práctica del graduación. No podría mover. Que linda fuiste. No tenía ningunas palabras. Yo solo podría mirarte. Más tarde, me pensé que yo tengo hacerlo. No queré nada más que hablar contigo; para congratularte; para decirte buén trabaja. Estoy orgulloso de ti. Estoy feliz por ti. Ya sabía que tenías un nuevo hombre para amar, y bueno, pero no seguré que si tendrías tu familia allá para apoyarte. Sonreí por eso.

No seguro si tú sabías que yo había visitado. Yo poné unas cartas en tú buzón. Quería que solo fueras feliz. Cuidé que no arruinar tú momento de triunfo. Quería que tu tener un momento perfecto para recordar, pero yo vi los pensamientos usuales escrito en tu cara. ¿Fue yo? ¿Estás pensando en mí ahora?

Yo recuerdo todos los cosas pequeñas hiciste por mi. Los grandes también. Todos en el medio. Todos que tomé por gratis. Que bendición fuiste por mi vida, y ahora también, incluso desde una distáncia.

Yo escribiendo esta carta en Español dondé Inglés ya me ha fallado. Es más apropiado en este lengua porque es más fácil ponerte delante de mí.

Me diste todos de ti, y no fui listo hacer lo mismo. Lo siento, mi corrazón. Por favór perdóname y ser un parte de mi vida otra vez.

175

Penitence
08122017

You aggravate me endlessly
Fill me with uncertainty
I vacillate so seamlessly
Between my love and hate for you

Which of us is unworthy?
Standing on my pedestal
From afar I seem up above you
But when I look back, you're
looking down

Will I ever know for sure?
If not, then let me find the cure
Day in, day out, I'm reeling 'round
You're all I think about

Imagining when next we meet
My heart sunk down beneath my
feet
Trying to express to you
The way you make me feel

The way you look is maddening
From whence it settled down
beneath
It's coming to a head

My hands full-up with all your skin
Your taste, it slithers deep within
Breathe out my air
I'm diving in, lost inside of you
again

Searching the sheets for sweet
release
Anxiety calling out for peace
Please twist and break, unravel me
Turn 'round so I can undo you

From so far away
I await the day
Our paths meet each other
And I meet your gaze

I may glance away
You might be gone
I may look back someday
What could have been

But am I good for you?
Are you good for me?
Can forgiveness come someday?

I think of only you
You're all I think about
You're clearly what I want
But I every time I start
I'm halfway in and stepping out

You consume my thoughts
It's clear you're what I need
The battles that I've fought
I can't show up for me

176

Drunken Dribble
08152017

I wasn't sure
I had to move on
You could have been the one
Now you're gone

If I'm not sure
I can't resolve
Can't seem to settle
Can't give my all

Day in
Day out
Moments marked between
Still feel much the same
Not sure what that means

I am where I am
You are where you are
I still long for your touch
Dwell on you from afar

Is past, past?
Is done, what is done?
I slither through people
Recanted by some

Step away from that crowd
Hold my hand with me here
For the first time sincere
Let me call you, "My Dear"

Dear Andrew & Breanna
09112017

Y'all,

Thank you so goddamn much for welcoming me into your fucking incredible ceremony. It was THE shit. This fucking wedding was not only a goddamn pleasure to be a part of, but it was also a fucking rite of passage into a new phase of life for me. Next level shit. This was my first wedding and first friend to get married and I'm just happy as a barrel of fucking pickles about it.

Thanks a shitton for having me and helping with the transit. Fucking thank you for putting me up. Thanks for the memories (Fall Out Boy). I look forward to the day I can return that fucking favor. Holy fuck. It's gonna be fuckin sweet. Yous guys are the perfect couple. The one whole and three teeth shit and all that.

On the real, such a fucking learning experience for me to see what all goes into a wedding and how to not fuck around. Way to do that shit. You did it. And it was fucking dope shit you can brag on for-fucking-ever. I'm glad I finally made it to New Hampshire what a goddamn motherfucking unreal fucking pleasure it was.

With love,
Costa

P.S. Why aren't you here rn? Wtf. Hurry the f*** up.

Collateral Intentions

An Introduction
09182017

Welcome to the Slam
Every person in this room is probably the most beautiful you have ever seen
Why?

Slam poetry is typically an emotional zit being popped
Come, the Open
The Broken and Abused
The Misused
Context
Sometimes stripped and superimposed
Much like these pieces of ourselves
Our personal hells and heavens assembled into
Mosaic glasses we peer through
Poetry slammed and peer-reviewed
Judge, validate, appreciate, evaluate

In this room
You will find for each pair of eyes, a pair of glasses
Shattered and remade
Seeking to be broken again
A few of us here relaying our observations on stage

Souls are intangible and life can be concrete
Bodies simple vessels sandblasted in heat
Glass doesn't hold up so well slammed against the street

Look around this room and you will find some of the most beautiful souls you
have ever witnessed
How?

Trade shades and you will see shadows cast
Demons-past echo in our ears
Blood on the page, smeared with tears, wrapt with laughs
Don't sweat it
You're gonna regret it
Your voice will be heard if you just let it

Glass breaks and is remade
Again
Welcome to the Slam

179

Don't Ask
09182017

I don't want you to ask
I just
Want you
To fucking
Do it

Goddamn we tried
And in spite of ourselves
We couldn't make us work

If I wasn't so stuck on how we fucked
If I didn't place so much stock in the way you sucked my cock

I'll admit
I was entranced every time we took off each other's pants
If it isn't clear: Goddamn that sex was good!
Maybe even love was made
And it's that fact that makes we wish I stayed

You never lied
Well, maybe once or twice I second-guessed
But let's not focus on that
We could make it because the third time's the charm
And I could change my mind again and hurt you a fourth time
Five, six, pick up sticks and stones
I feel you in my bones
And your words are what adorn my crown
Let me have that attention again
Let me never question again

But why did I even doubt in the first place?
You fanned the flames of my extremes
So deniably in, so undeniably out
Our roller coaster made my gut roll
My gut pushed me away for a reason
But I do have a sensitive stomach
Maybe things will be different next time

Oh yeah, what about getting exhausted trying to fix you?
Oh yeah, what about the way I threw my responsibilities on you?
Oh yeah, what about the way you took the opportunity to rebound the next day
when we broke up the first time, not once, not twice, but five, six, pick up sticks
I'm gonna be sick
I'm gonna be sick

Beauty, clarity, guilt, praise, pleasure, pain
These are a few of my favorite things
But are you the whole of my love, or are you the zero-sum total of its parts?

Denver Calling
09252017

I may grow weary of Denver, yet
The lights flicker
The sun burns
The wind cuts
The shadows grow and the snow freezes
Things come and go and stay for a reason or a season
And I am one of those

Denver calling
I answer
There may be a new call not too far off
But I am enjoying this time
Durango is uncharted

There may be wild oats, yet
I've planted seeds in Denver
My roots are tepid and feeling for warm, nourishing soil
Thank you for this
Thank you for all I have to remember and all I have yet to forget

I feel my fortune well beyond anything I am owed
And I am overcome
What a blessing
What a blessing
What a beautiful story
The mountain is high
It's peak gazing down
I have already seen so much
Maybe its triumph will even bring the ocean in view

Projects
10032017

Abandoned things always feel special
Because they feel like they're left just for you
Falling apart in their own pretty way

Everybody else walks by not seeming to notice
You start thinking of the possibilities
How you could fix it back up again
How you could stain it with your blood, sweat, and tears
Nobody else to tell you wrong from right
Or good or bad

It could be your own
It could be for free
Come back to it in the morning
And come back at night
Heart pounding
When you pass by the "No Trespassing" sign to get inside
To see all its angles in a different light

And maybe I'm talking about broken buildings
And maybe I'm thinking about you and me

Rewritten
10152017

You put a screen in every hand of a generation
You take a chance to explore different avenues
Nothing is the seed of something
And when there is always something drawing your attention
A generation ends-up doing nothing
When nothing is private
There's always something to talk about
But a generation ends-up saying nothing

There is no going back
There was a time for this-or-that
It wasn't so this
And that is so much more than it ever was
I don't know about this and
I just don't understand that

You adapt or you die
Before it was written
It was spoken
Now it's encoded
We broke our genetic sequence
The future is ours to be molded
Where will you be
When the possibilities are reloaded?

Dear Feminism
11192017

I want to talk about feminism.

Now, whether you're already deeply entrenched, or it's all brand new to you; it's a cause, it's a movement, it's a fight, and the front lines are everywhere. You will have umpteen opportunities to fight for the cause. I have something to say about it because I–personally–am male. Particularly, a white, cis-gendered, heterosexual, mesomorphic male. I represent enemy and ally #1 in America.

As it stands, we men hold the injustices for which feminism is founded on. Now, it is everyone's movement–for women–but, as an ally, I want to share my perspective. In a highly publicized (often skewed) political climate, men have umpteen opportunities to feel threatened by the label, "feminism." Many of our slights against women often come from an inability to experience reality as a woman and unconscious patterns that are culturally and socially ingrained, informing the basis of our reality. There are men/people who are just too-far-gone, but for those of us just living life based on our informed (or uninformed) reality: we need inspiration, not isolation.

Let's *please* pick our battles, make the conversation fit the comment, and remember that feminism means different things to different people. If we project the entire weight of all of our personal experiences onto a single person, moment, comment, or injustice, the battle is already lost.

Everyone has a forest of experiences and beliefs through which they walk and live. If we come in trying to uproot somebody's entire forest which they spent their lives nourishing and living in, they won't let it happen. However, if we plant seeds, those seeds can slowly grow, integrate, and overtake a forest. There are different levels of severity in each instance and battle, so let's use our discretion; Is this an instance where a person's tree needs chopping down or will planting a seed do?

The kind of change we're working toward is under a thick canopy of preconceptions. It takes time. There is already a fire burning, clearing out the old to make way for the new, and if we aren't patient in how we plant these new ideas, we will burn each other, and the same old growth will come back.

Love,
Constantine

Third Shift "I Feel"
01082018

   3 shifts deep so far...I *fucking love* my dream job. I feel useful. I feel accomplished. I feel fulfilled. I feel this way when I get feedback that I'm doing great and making connections with awesome co-workers. I believe I feel this way because I set a goal of becoming a wilderness therapy field guide a few years ago and made deliberate progress to achieve that goal. I also believe I feel this way because I've struggled in the past to make connections and friends in new places. My intention for myself is to be cognizant of investment and burnout. My request for everyone else is to give me high-fives.

Billy Colfax (by Bluebird Adams)
11272017

Your latest right swipe is waiting a few blocks up Colfax at some "best hole-in-the-wall" place with the "best in town" whatever.

"Excuse me, Lord, excuse me, may I tell you my best pun?" A voice pleads.

He could just feed you some shit about a specific amount of money he's conveniently short for the bus, or motel, or food. He could sit, shaking a cup, or stand with a sign depicting something pitiful, or cliché, or witty, like "Anything Helps," "God Bless," or "Green is Good!" But this is a booming metropolis. Every busy corner has a scheduled rotation of panhandlers with their own angle on it. Billy is offering a service: interactive insights.

"No time. Sorry." Your stride, unbroken.

He maneuvers around you. "How about my best truth? Two dollars if it's bad, five if it's bangin'," Billy bargains.

When you finally meet his gaze, you're greeted by the ash of his skin, the gray of his hair, the hoarse of his voice, and the edge of his wit. You've seen him before. He's "lived" here for years. Billy has come to embody the street which he inhabits. He keeps one eye covered with a pirate's patch to preserve his night vision, ready to defend against creatures of the night (plus it looks cool and can pull a few extra bucks here and there). Due to Billy's housing flexibility and spaded peers, his possessions are fleeting. He keeps his most sacred treasures incanted upon memory-lock: words of his own, his idol (Prince), and his lord and savior (God). With these, Billy regales the abiding passerby with a litany of laughs, lunacy, or liturgy. His fearless attitude is an ode to the legacy of hustlers, transients, and rebels that's earned Colfax a reputation for warding off prey and welcoming predators.

You weigh your options in a half-step: at least you'll have an opening story for your date and an excuse for being late.

You huff, "Fine, hit me."

His body curls into itself, lowering towards the ground.

You begin to wish you'd kept walking.

He explodes into the air, "The best way to get over someone—"

Returning to earth uncomfortably close to you with a flat-footed slap, he stabs his hand between your shins and cocks his gaze through your legs down Colfax for a moment, "—is to get under another!"

You pull in a breath, finding your arms wrapped in defense against the knife you were sure he had.

Breaking statue, he looks up to you and steps back, raising his arms to the sunset's afterglow, "And as Solomon wrote—!"

"Billy!" You interrupt.

"What's up?" Arms still afloat.

"One's enough."

"Alright. So?"

"Bangin'," as you draw your cash.

Billy's hand crumples the five in yours, and his eye wanders to another victim. "Excuse me, M'lady, may I trouble you for a moment of your time?"

You're now 15 minutes late and frantically tapping through apps to recall which one you matched with so you can remember who and where you're meeting.

Predisposition
12042017

On the second Millenniversary in the year of our Lord, there came a generation; some just born, some already coming into their own. It had been 2,000 years since the new era began, marked not by the birth of a messiah but the death of one. In turn, 2,000 years of war, evolution, and industry rotted the psyche of the young American.

These were the finest the human race had to offer; their DNA packed with genetic memories of all its people had been through. The previous generations envied this. They envied their youth. They envied their freedom. They envied their possibilities and potential. This deep-seated disdain manifested itself as it usually does: criticizing others for our own faults which we are either unwilling or unable to change.

Entitled. Delicate. Lazy. Selfish. Disrespectful. Spoiled. Impulsive. Naïve. Impractical. Stupid.

When someone tells you something enough, you begin to believe it. They adopted the role their ancestors prescribed. In fact, any deviation from tradition was damned as regression. As each transgressive label piled against each new actor and seed of thought, the new generation became gaslit into confusion. To name these labels for what they were was seen as arrogant, an act of transgression in itself. Arguments became circular. Fact became fiction and vice versa. It seemed everyone was doing wrong in someone's eyes.

Growth is often painful, often met with resistance. For a cell to divide, its most basic foundations must first be shaken into complete chaos. Though they are in essence an exact copy of one another, one is still a newer version. They're ultimately working towards the same goal, duplicated to carry out the same exact tasks as those before them. However, with each iteration, each new growth, comes opportunity. If the change is too radical too soon, it becomes cancerous. The cancer will either be eradicated to preserve the original living systems, or it will spread and destroy that which it was charged with preserving. Occasional iterations of small mutations are allowed, so long as they serve their original purpose under the supervision and authority of their ancestors. Over time, the small changes go unnoticed or undeterred. All generations become old habits, old actions, old thoughts, then die. Stress is nature's fulcrum of evolution, but it is ambition which tips the scales.

As these millennials matured, they began taking sides. For some, the old ways worked. They became obedient, militant copies of their forefathers. Others questioned their charge at birth and wondered if their lives were meant not just to perpetuate, but to improve. It is worth noting that millennials were not the first to envision more for themselves and the cells around them, but divergent thought reached a cancerous fulcrum. At this point in history, the scales needed only be tipped by ambition: that of the old or that of the new.

2,000 years ago marked the birth of a harbinger, but the new era did not begin until after his death.

Reflections on Volume IX

Almost to the end! You're doing great! What a journey we've been on! Remember that time you wandered aimlessly through a book about a stranger's life, reflecting on your own? What a time, am I right? You need anything? Cup of tea? Stretch break? It's best to finish strong, you know.

"Life is a Sketch" takes place in 2016, 2017, and 2018; ages 25 to 26. It picks up in the heat of my homecoming as a different person. Everything was the same, and everything was different. I'd been places, seen and done things that kept me slightly more removed than I was before I left and itching to leave again.

I made another friend while working overnights at Home Depot. I attended my first wedding as an adult for a best friend from home (as a groomsman, no less!). My mom finished her battle with breast cancer. I started ordering a bunch of crap from Wish.com (which was a big deal for me because I was a tight-ass with money and rarely treated myself). I connected with more women. I bought a car (RIP Francesca: Barcelona Red, 2008 Toyota RAV4 Unicorn, totaled in a head-on sideswipe on Wolf Creek Pass).

I met a girl that brought healing into my life. We spent time together whenever I had a moment to spare, which was rare. We rescued a baby blue jay thrashing by one leg, caught in fishing line from its nest. I enjoyed another summer love. We didn't jump into a relationship because my knee was healing and I planned on getting out of Florida immediately. Enter: A City Year alum looking for a roommate in Denver.

Peace out once again, Florida. I built her a tire swing in her front yard and hit the road. I took my time traveling across the middle of the U.S. back to Denver. Over the span of two weeks, I camped at a dozen different state and national parks and made a fun road trip video to chronicle my solo adventure. I enjoyed some inner peace and excitement about the prospect of getting back on track with my dream job. I transferred jobs with Home Depot (this time to a day job in the paint department), worked for Denver Parks and Recreation doing after-school programming, and drove for Lyft in between. Once again, the grind was on, and I could not be stopped. I got a short story ("Smile") published in an indie art magazine in Denver and made my first $25 as a writer (the check is still framed next to the centerfold, uncashed). This was my second chance to explore Denver and make new friends but my 26th birthday was another rough one I spent alone. I applied to the Open Sky Wilderness and they invited me to orientation.

I made it to Durango, CO. My instructors were inspirationally weird and shared a rock through each of their digestive tracts (I would later carry this torch). Guiding challenged me in new ways and gave me opportunities to coalesce all the skills and tools I had gathered in my previous years. I felt an incredible sense of accomplishment, purpose, and community. I made a new friend. We instantly connected, both got the job, moved in together, and basically spent every waking moment together. We went to Mexico for both our first times. We landed in Cancun and bussed our way around the peninsula. I fell in love (lust) with a stripper. We flew across the mainland—the sickest we've been in our lives—and spent 48 hours in bed at a hostel, took a ferry to Baja California, and hitchhiked all the way up to Tijuana, where we crossed the border on foot.

I retreated into a bit of a writing pause in this section, reflecting more and generating less, hence three years packed into one journal. Near the end of this volume, I realized I had a decade's worth of creative pieces strewn across ten journals, and I decided to start compiling them into one neat collection.

Forever
Just passing through

I am here
Right now
And I am at peace//

Volume
/////X/////

Black
n'
Red

01092018

//

110 2019

Ages

1,335 Days
01092018

It's been nearly 3 years and 8 months since we said yes to each other in Tijuana Flats: May 7, 2014, 19:41 PM. It's hard to believe you've been on my mind and in my heart for 1,335 days, already. Tonight, I found my way through my journals and—inevitably—back to those times, those thoughts and feelings.

I'm still stirred restless by you. I still don't know if we could or should or would work, but every night I'm left with the thought of your love and what it means to me. Being so torn is unbearable. I would love so much to have tea with you and see who you've become and what you've done with your time. I wonder if either of us has really changed or done much growing.

Any love, regret, longing, desire, lust, and discontent I have for you runs deep in me. I've learned to work next to these things and done well for myself, but they remain in some part of anything I do. I think, in that, they are your blessings to me. I feel them with a fond tenderness, and it feels like you. You were so good to me, healed me, gently pushed and carried me on my way. I wonder if I'll ever be able to make room for you or someone like you in my life and doubting that hurts.

I'm baffled by my ability to endure and my inability to accept and move on. You are so beautiful and warm. Thank you so much for the gift of you. I hope to see you soon.

All my love,
Constantine

Folding Mountains
01232018

There comes a time when city lights are replaced
By the raw energy of fire wrapt 'round logs
Chewing them up
Accelerating their molecular bodies
Into the ash of the future
Sending dancing smoke
Into billion-year-old light beams
Of sparkling galaxies o'erhead
A time when the earth rises to meet us
The wind whispers hello
And rivers carve through our hardened insecurities
In these times, we come to know our ancestors
In these times, we meet the origin of the soul

Home for the Holidays
03052018

Keep your head lifted and you will be lifted up.

Fears keep you alive, but they also keep you from living.

Art will keep and restore your youth.

Inside my straw
A pleasant ding introduces
Red X over a cigarette
Green play button between a seatbelt

Elbows dig into the wind
My chair pulls me into my seat
Turbines whir whispers in my ear
Of lands afar and seas beneath

All is upright and secured
The ground shrinking
Not saying goodbye
Just saying, "See you soon"

Christmas lights spill over the ground
Some still freshly folded in their packaging
The neurons of a city fire across highways in headlights pairs
Dark matter isolates select memory clusters

When was the last time you were lifted up?

Guide Me (for Eli)
07312018

I find myself
No
I find myself thinking
No
I find myself by thinking
No
I thought I found myself
But there it goes
And I don't know again
I lost my mind
To find my heart in shards
Departed from everything I knew
You, you, you
Is all I could do
So when I busted my first "I Feel"
I felt strangely…myself

But fuck these trees
Fuck therapy
Fuck this mental dis-ease
ADHD, Anxiety, PTSD, Label Me

You don't know me
You don't own me
You don't care about me
So leave me be

I'm lost
And I don't care to wander
aimlessly
Over this hill
Through these woods
Another pill down we go

Popping pills
Coping skills
Chasing thrills
These "I Feels"
Are driving me up a fucking wall
That doesn't even exist

Because I am stuck in the middle of
Wilderness
Therapy
Incapable of escaping
Incapable of erasing
Incapable of deciding the next step
in my life

Because my old choices brought me
One step away from death
Or worse

Turn the page
For a new chapter
Not the hereafter
Not the end
But to begin, again

To not only choose life
But choose to live
To give more and take less
To cope with stress
Maybe not the best
Not yet
But better
Today
Here
Now

In this moment
I find myself
Maybe lost the next
I accept that
And love me nonetheless
And all the more
Tomorrow

Inheritance
08042018

To whom it may concern,

Year: 2064. Earth's population passes 10,000,000,000,000, and 99.9% of the world's wealth is held by less than 0.0000001% of the population: "The 1K." The other 99.9999999% survives in a state of placated drollity and moderate strife to varying degrees but a narrow range.

How did we get here? What can we do about it?

Generations climbed over each other's warnings. Each saw first-hand what was happening, either knowing the urgency but placing hope in the next generation—disillusioned with powerlessness—or the next accepting the apparent declination as all they ever knew, not yet aware of how much worse things had truly become and how much momentum was building. In between these lapses of action and judgement were those small windows of realization and initiation, fractured by the inability to agree and organize. Meanwhile, the scales continued to tip as fortunes were absorbed, consolidated, and inherited into the now "1K."

There was once power in unions and strikes, but their effect was nullified as the revolving door of a desperate workforce built the machines which automated and antiquated their position of power. Boycotts reached a point of diminishing returns as the diversity of goods and services simultaneously narrowed, while pre-automation methods of self-reliance became all-but-extinct. National sovereignty dissolved parallel to corporate mergers, resulting in cultural brackishing until it reached homeostasis, in which sedimentary pillars of pride, values, and community were replaced with the granite slab of corporate agenda. The remaining global conglomerates attained a near-perfect ratio of production to the consumption of capital. The rest has been simply witnessing the clash of corporate titans inching past each other to take one another out until... well... what, exactly?

There is one final throne for the second-closest to continuously usurp in the last and greatest revolving door of absolute power, until finally there comes one benevolent ruler to masterfully dismantle the final reflection of our own latency, so we may once again have a chance at redemption in the hopes that we may act quickly enough to sustain their efforts before they fall victim to their own mortality, leaving the chance for limitless power to tempt another?

...right.

History can teach us a great many things, but it cannot make a horse drink. How do I know all this? I was there, and—like you—I accepted the leftovers of my ancestors to the best of my own complicit pleasure. I didn't care for the discomfort of confronting my peers—or for that matter, myself—to stand up, and I handed the burden on to those who succeeded my personal failure, so they may carry on our tradition.

This is the moment I grew up hearing, "It's up to you now. I've done all I can." But somehow, here we are, and I'm still writing you this letter.

Enjoy the Harvest
08082018

At the ranch, ready and waiting to go into the field. Today we have yoga and swimming in Summit Lake for our in-service. This fits with the positive trend lately. I had my second therapy session with Kendall yesterday and she helped me reflect on the idea that—maybe for the first time in my life—all cylinders are firing: socially, emotionally, financially(ish), intimately, professionally, platonically, personally. I have a strong community of friends I can rely on. I'm open to my emotions and dealing with them in healthy ways. I'm making enough money to sustain myself and set a small bit aside while lowering my debt. I have women in my life that I'm interested in and are consistent. I'm moving up in work and I feel accomplished, proud, and fulfilled by my dream job while working to find my next logical step. My relationship with my father is the strongest it's ever been and I stay decently in touch with my close friends and family. I just read and dissected nearly 10 years of journals to gather my creative works and reflect on who I've been, who I am now, and who I would like to become. I am currently working in my Xth journal with the intention of writing more, writing more regularly, and endorsing a more visible maturity. My new home is signed for a year of renting and all my room is moved-in and settled. We have solos this week in Kudu on the Black Mesa Loop. My goal is to get all the rest of my guide pathway knocked-out and ready to start shadowing for senior by the first shift in September, get out to my third therapy session with Kendall the following Thursday to process, then enjoy and reflect on my shift-off so I can come back for a few more senior shadow shifts in October and officially senior for my 1-year anniversary in November! I'll senior through Thanksgiving, then go home for a month in December for Christmas. Maybe then I'll find some time to work on concrete next steps in the coming year, 5 years, and 10 years, also time to relax, unplug, decompress, recharge, and reunite with loved ones, of course.

For now, I'm overcome with feeling blessed. I deserve this time, these blessings, this love, and these opportunities. Hard work does pay-off. My 27th year has been a return on investments. In 17 days, I will enter my 28th year, when I hope to capitalize on these returns with plans to re-invest. Enjoy the harvest, my friend, you've earned it.

Durga Time Capsule
10042018

Here we are
Lost and Found
Here we are
Mighty and Willing
Here we are
Reluctantly in Love
Here we are
More than the Sum of our Mistakes
We are the Grand Total of our Potential

Our depths are as deep as we dive
We learn to live under pressure
We learn to come up for air
When to extend a hand for help
Here we are
And here we learn

Desert Awakening (by Team Durga)
11272018

Desert sands drip through the hourglass
Each granule, a moment of awakening
The sands of time blowing you by
Thousands of years to carve this canyon
And a million years for the rock to form

Inquisitively, I stood there in awe, gazing
Body swaying
I believe in this sight
You may shake your head
But I believe I am right
To stand up for a cause
And strive to be better
And strive to be braver
And strive to be wiser

As the arms of the willow
Reach toward the ground
Brushing their knowledge across your brow

So, I exclaimed in a course tone:
"Sometimes people don't think it be like it is, but it do!"
Do, do, do, do, do
Yes! Yes! No. Yes!
I change my mind often
But I digress

We are the best
And that's no joke
Laughing under winter's snowflake kisses
Wrapt in desert warmth by day
Greeted by the moon at night
Basking in its dark, knowledgeable light

The light—at first glance—seemed dim
After a closer look
I noticed a shining star
The color was clear
The color is true
And that is all for us
This poem is through

Wet Windows
12032018

All is right
When the world seems wrong

Chest is tight
Devil singing a song

What is this feeling
When I have nothing to fear

What is healing
When wounds blood-let tears

Mistakes of the past
Lessons in love

I call to the rain
Answers down from above

The Hard Work is in the Heart Work
12032018

Eyes freshly swollen
Blood gathering around them
To pump out
What I've been holding in

I see you
Maybe for the first time
At least
As far as I can remember

I hope some of this blood
Works it's way into my brain
And wrinkles in a landmark
So in its valley, I can look up
To the cranial canyon walls
And find petroglyphs of this moment

The salt dried on my face
I could have carried from an ocean breeze held in
From coast to mountain home
Which you brought with you on your visit

You shared something for the first time
A last request
If not in life
That I will be carried into death
In the breast pocket of my namesake

Hereafter, this reunion awaits yet another goodbye
Although it always could have been sooner
I'm glad this relief comes sooner
Rather than later
Rather than too late
Better than not at all
As it was for you and your father

Paragon
12162018

We build monuments to immortalize something of meaning
Pyramids rise and fall before me
But the intention is lost in translation
Leaving others only to guess in the windfall of the hourglass

What timeless message we were trying to capture
To convey
Remember this
Time can be a lapse of judgement

Perhaps that segregation of origin is for the better
Spurring us into education so we can make educated guesses
Building a monument of research we could collectively agree on
The true monument:
          Agreement
Perhaps that is the message of the ages

I spent my entire life building something I would never finish
So that you could remember this
I believed in the power of our message
So that you could remember this
No matter what you do, remember this:

We are better when we come together

Perhaps it is sometimes best to let history fall to the sands
So that we can envision a brighter tomorrow
Time can be a lapse of judgement

Halfway
12282018

How long can I reach out?
Before my arm gets tired
Every time I do
The muscles get stronger

I don't want to go back
To what we had
It didn't feel right
Doesn't feel right now
But it felt wrong
Still feels wrong
I just want to right that wrong
To move on

But what can I do?
If you won't meet me halfway
To hear what I have to say
At least keep moving
And meet myself where I'm at

I wish the best for you
And for me
And that's that

Swipe
01072019

You've run out of likes! Buy 100 more likes for just $2.99. Click-out. Open the next app. There's no one new in your area! Go to settings to extend your range! You've already set your maximum distance! You've run out of apps! You've run out of options! Go to a shady bar during happy hour and increase your chances! Domestics are two for one!

The other day I found everything I was looking for but nothing I was interested in. Looking back, I realize I had 20 things I wanted, and 20 things that I forgot I hated.

I keep a list of girls in my head who made me cum. It's the most amazing thing.

I asked them, "Where did you learn that?"
They mutter something and I reply, "Don't talk with your mouth full."
I keep a list of girls in my head that couldn't make me cum.
And when I didn't they asked me, "How come?"
I told them, "It's hard to understand, but I'll keep asking."

I cut my emotions off at the knees, otherwise they might kick me where I would feel it. Otherwise, I might realize the dread of trying to swipe my way to happiness. Otherwise, I might recognize the irony that a smartphone makes a mind dumb and a heart careless. Otherwise, I might enjoy these dates and this sex and the way your face matches your name in my memory that represents something that I'm actually invested in.

Maybe it's wise to do it the other way, but how stupid could I be to actually acknowledge my feelings? I would rather them sit on the other side of a couch, me with my arms crossed, having somebody else analyze them instead of myself.

I would sooner tell you that I love you than tell you the passcode to my phone.

Now, hurry up, finish me off, and leave me the fuck alone.

One in a Million
01072019

Lonely-ass people
Staying high to forget
Missing people I haven't met
Walking alone at night

Smoking my cheap cigars
Drinking PBR in five bars
Becoming a million different
people
At the same time

Wandering through the streets
Visiting different countries
Imagining another life
Everywhere I set my feet

New paces with old places
Trading knives for playing cards
Giving up my bones for new guitars
Sweaters hang in my closet

When I find someone I like
I get ahead of myself
Imagining by myself
The fights we'd have down the road

Maybe I'm drawn to distinction
There's no resolution in sight
The light's too bright
So I go to sleep at dawn

Depression goes undiagnosed
Hold my anxiety cuts too close
Take a last breath
A cloud of smoke
Get to the end
Backtrack
Walk it all again

All these lonely ass people
Looking for a friend
No one to pick up the phone
So we just pretend

There's someone on the other line
When we post to the internet ghost
Demons come up to haunt us
When we're losing control

Finding out as I get older
My loneliness complex
Is directly proportionate
To the number of faces I fuck in
bed

I'm a million different people
Being everybody and nobody
At the same damn time
Lonely ass people walk the streets
at night

206

Near Miss
01172019

Somewhere far way
She's just laying there
Sheets are tossed like her short hair
Beside the one she confides in

Somewhere far away
I'm just sitting here
Thinking of the nights we shared
Wishing I could go back to her

This night will pass like all of the rest
Remembering
How shirts would hold her chest
How she was better than the best

Some come and go
My bed gets cold again
My love for her
Remains the same

I saw her tears
I see her smile now
Look back and wonder how
How could I betray our hearts

Somewhere far away
She's sitting next to me
I'm begging her to forgive me
A day away, an eternity

CHORDS
Am
Dm
F
G

CHORUS
D
C
B

Bobby & Emily's Wedding Speech
03232019

In 2016, Date Lab Matchmaker and freelance writer Christina Breda Antoniades pursued the secret to a long-lasting marriage. These are her findings, published in the Washington Post:

"They've accomplished a feat almost everyone who ties the knot aspires to: to reach old age together, glad they picked each other. They've shared life's happiest moments but also weathered its biggest challenges. A happy, long-term union—the experts seem to agree—hinges in part on pairing-up wisely and in part on mastering the skills that foster a healthy marriage.

They work hard to master effective communication - not just talking but listening, and such couples make generosity and kindness habitual, committing small acts of service, like cleaning up without being asked. They're willing to forgive their spouse's faults and failings. They treat each other with respect.

There's one other thing long-married couples devote effort to: keeping their marriage interesting. Even after decades together, they carve out time as a couple, take an interest in each other's passions and take steps to foster intimacy. Equally important is choosing—and of course being—a solid life partner: reliable, responsible, and honest are a good start. It helps, too, to pick a mate who is resilient in the face of life's curveballs, says Pepper Schwartz, a sociologist, and AARP's relationships expert, "Someone who will go, 'Okay, this is the new normal; let's figure it out,' or, 'This is exciting, let's have an adventure!'"

I've heard quite a bit that, "getting old ain't no fun." You're walking into a lifetime commitment to have fun together, and the older you get, the tougher it can be to adapt to new norms and seek adventure.

There will come a time when you won't be able to lay shoulder-to-shoulder with a best friend on a card table-sized floatation device, rowing with palm fronds through a canal of mating stingrays and jellyfish. There will come a time when you won't be able to hold each other up for keg stands and "shot-for-shot" becomes a conversation about your trips to the doctor instead of trying to piece a story together about last night that you (mostly) remember.

There will come a time when you each will need a helping hand, like when you get ticks in hard-to-reach places while primitive camping in Ocala. There will come a time when you may be able to float up 800 feet in the air behind a boat, but probably skip the part when you get dragged through the water like rag dolls at 30 knots. There will come a time when you will again sit on your ass all day on the back porch and start to wonder where the time went as the sun sets. When those times come, I hope you don't give it a second thought because they were spent with the one you love.

When times get tough, you may get so mad the two of you want to kill each other, so make sure you watch all the episodes of CSI: Miami and Murder Mysteries together so the other doesn't get the upper hand, pretend you still love each other so the other doesn't catch on, and plan an elaborate getaway to a far-off destination, but no cruises, too many witnesses.

When I heard Bobby stood (rather, knelt) in the fire of his fear of heights to propose to Emily, I knew he was committed to working on himself so he could be the best man he could for her. It's important to take time for yourself to reflect on who you are and how you're growing as a person when you come together as one. As you two transition from two pasts apart into your future together, remember: whether you're researching what the experts say about longevity, diving into an adventure you know you're going to regret immediately, or plotting an intricate homicide, you promise to respect, support, and share your lives with one another.

Best Man
03182019

I'm going to my best friend's wedding and all I can think about is how little time I've spent in relationships, how much time I've spent out of them, how confusing and challenging it is for me to meet someone I'm interested in, and how hopeless and powerless I feel to change that.

Happy Young Couple Not Actually A Couple and Not That Happy
05112019

In a world where the girl or guy next door can be as close as the maximum distance in your dating app settings, what's the use in settling down? We live in a time when dating has been optimized into a business transaction. With dating apps like Tinder and Bumble, it's easier than ever to find people in your area and ask for pics. So easy, in fact, that most apps impose a cap on how many people you can like per day.

At the same time, this increased connectivity has somehow wedged a communication crutch into the dating world such that people are afraid to interact in any form that isn't digital. With so many options available, it's easy to match with someone and still have reservations for that next "perfect someone." Enter: the Nonrel. Nonrel is short for "non-relationship"; a commitment to stay in touch and not commit to each other.

To get the inside scoop on the under-workings of this new-wave dating revolution, two fully non-committed non-trepreneurs in a nine-month nonrel, Zac (27) and Alice (26), agreed to chat with us online, separately.

Q: So how did you two meet?
Zac: It all started when we matched on Tinder. I agonized over the perfect opener to let her know my intentions and get a response. I settled on, "Hey." Next thing I know, I ask her out, she agrees, then says she can't make it the night of [our date(s)]. So we try a couple more times. No luck. We end up saying, "Hey, let's just commit to not commit," and here we are!
Alice: We matched. He messaged the same old boring stuff, but I really liked his picture with his cat, so I agreed to go on a couple dates, but every time it came down to it, I was just like, "Why bother?" You know? Anyways, he's cute and sweet and I like the attention.

Q: Do you know anybody else in a nonrel?
Alice: Totally! After about two months, my friends kept asking about Zac and I. "Are you still talking to that guy?" And I would tell them, "Sort of, not really, but yeah." They were fascinated and wanted to give it a try.
Zac: Oh, tons! I told all my friends all about it and they started scrolling through old matches they never started a chat with. Now, they're all completely non-committal!

Q: What is the hardest part of being in a nonrel?
Alice: I'd say it's challenging to stay open to other possibilities. Once you're committed to not commit, then you're committed, you know what I mean?
Q: ...no...
Alice: It's like, we check in on each other for birthdays, holidays, always making plans that we can cancel. Then when one of us finds someone else we're interested in, it's like, "I don't know if I have time in my schedule to make and cancel all these plans with even more people!"
Zac: I think the hardest part is just trying to manage it all while trying to save time for yourself. I find myself shopping for flowers, looking up Groupons for date night, knowing I'm going to cancel at the last confirmation page on PayPal. It's really time-consuming.

Q: What's your favorite date you've turned down?

Alice: Definitely the all-inclusive trip to the Caymans. Zac found this fantastic Groupon for a cruise, cabana, scooter rentals, and a one-night, six-course meal! I was so into it, but I just couldn't!

Zac: Oh man, probably Alice's idea to go to this huge underground rave, except we would stay on opposite sides of the crowd all night! I liked it so much I turned her down and I went anyway—don't tell her!

Q: Where do you see the two of you going in the future?

Zac: Oh man, what a question! It's really hard to say. I probably couldn't, even if I tried. I don't know. I really like some of her ideas I get to turn down, and she likes turning mine down, too. Maybe we'll break it off and not commit to other people. Who knows?

Alice: Wow! Yeah, we're coming up on our one-year noniversary, so it's hard to say. Something like a "noniversary" seems too official. To be honest, we have discussed rejecting each other's wedding proposals. We're just not sure if we're ready for that kind of thing.

We got in touch with Zac and Alice post their one-year noniversary to see how things panned out for them. We set a date and time that worked for everyone, but both could not make it to the chat. They have not followed up with us since.

Old Man's Beard
05232019

Spring is a gathering of energies ·
The smothering providence of tempests
Relentless gentle drops worming into every crevice
Lightning rakes till the soil into moist fires

The sky droops with water weight
Draped over mountain banisters
Leaking rivulets into valleys
Collecting in mucky marsh buckets

Newborn, neon green dermis
Pushes out of age-hardened bark
The tender, spongey foliage
Absorbs the amniotic air

When the sun wrenches clouds apart
The forest sweats
Breathing fog
Condensing on the blue-sky windowpane

Change becomes a memory of itself; more than I can swallow in the world around
me. For now, the inevitable and ineffable change of youth is ephemeral and
therefore something to indulge in.

Dear Senioritis
08012019

Good morning, world!

It's overcast today with a 20% chance of rain: perfect conditions for AEGIS training outside. I'm waking-up in a comfortable sloth as the traffic outside whizzes, grumbles, and roars in my window. This is my second shift of feeling relief, contentedness, excitement, and confidence. I wonder if this is the emotional break I've been waiting for and its finally paying off in my patience. Maybe this is the sweet spot that's "3x sweeter as a senior than as a second," that I've been told about. Regardless, I'm grateful for reprieve in any form or duration. Some things I believe are contributing to this: more time off, achieving Senior 2, more adventures in my off time, mentoring other guides, mentoring other seniors (so I'm less-directly involved with holding the week), looking forward to the symposium, doing something I normally wouldn't do: swallow my pride and apologize to Cam, more massages/self-care, having Reiki done on me, time, working on validating my own growth, working on being more patient and present and buying myself little presents and enjoying the little extra money I'm making. Well, I'm off to breakfast. I hope this feeling stays a while.

Good work, Constantine.
You're doing a good thing for the world and for yourself. I'm proud of you, the work you're doing, and the man you're becoming.

Consolidated Feedback from the Field (Senior I - Senior II)
08152019

Positive

+ Rapport, presence, vision, individual and group awareness, passion
+ Incorporating therapeutic vision, guide development, attention to therapeutic detail, care for guides, pushing students
+ Grounded in crisis, made space for co-guide, relationship repair
+ Self-compassion, 1-on-1 check-ins, strong integrity, vulnerability
+ High value of debriefing hold with student and guide, supporting co-guide, clear communication, taking risk in relationship
+ Self-compassion, calm presence influencing students, high expectations, in-the-moment feedback, pushing students
+ Balancing play, structure and clear expectations to create a safe space for students and guides, less rigid, guide mentorship, consistent compassionate communication
+ High flexibility with plans changing, collaborating with guide team, caring for guides, emotional isomorphism, managing complex logistics
+ Emotional check-ins with guides, less intensity, managing a run situation, using Base time to complete paperwork, making space for guides, strong reflections to students
+ Mediated conflict resolution between students, moments of self-care, emotional check-ins with guides
+ Collaborating with 4 senior guides, calm management of crises, fun to work with, high competence, pushing students, guide mentorship

Constructive

- Communicate vision more, label behavior instead of character, find a "heart of peace" in conflict, clearly communicate boundaries
- Time management, front-loading group for consistencies for the week
- Black & white opinions, more motivational interviewing, wake-up earlier, use skills to avoid/prevent holds, narrate when rescuing students, struggled with self-confidence, manage expectations, relax (esp. with time management)
- Manage tone when driving students, hikes were too long, changed itinerary multiple times due to poor planning
- Be aware of tone and body language when offering challenging reflections to students, check-in with students 1-on-1 after breaking relationship with boundaries, etc.
- Prepare gear properly for weather, be aware of tone when de-escalating, communicate vision
- Find source & solution to burnout
- Senior stays with the team in crisis, slow to build rapport with group, manage intimidating energy

Open Mic at the Chicken Palace
09162019

His bony fingers
Choke the neck of a guitar

His foot taps every other strum of the strings

A reddish halo surrounds his ginger hair

The soft lamp light
Holds up his lyric journal

A candle by his foot
Dares the audience to watch it

Another sip of beer

A friend from the crowd
A duet is born
Before friction fire
His guitar sings along
With female harmony

The front porch sways
Looking-on to the neon signs afar
An electrical umbilical cord
Connects onlookers
And divides performance from audience

Heredity of Kairos
09282019

Night clouds blush
Upon being exposed
Morning sun and shadow
Stripe the earth

A meadow sings
Contentment by songbird
Preening its feathers
For the lone observer

Single trees
Stand in forest
Before their leaves
Prime into parchment

Still soft and supple
As tanned deer hide
They tell the grass
Of seasons past

Mealsome trunks squelch underfoot
Digesting in death
On the forest floor
Feeding the trees of tomorrow

Dirt and discarded needles
Yield to boulder and lichen
Valleys yawn open
Baring mountain teeth

Their morning breath
Rises from the void
Awakening drops of sweat
Resting on my skin

Ridgelines broil in Autumn hues
Slithering between prominences
As thunderous stomps
March down from above

The sun melts leaves
Into drops of shade
Draining into pools
Into rapids
Drawn into coniferous undertow

High noon heat
Stuffs my ears with cotton
Muffling cries of chattering insects
Beckoning the blanket of night

Wind pours canopies
Into roaring waterfalls
I wash ashore
My fireside refuge

I read bedtime stories
To the pregnant moon
Stars occasionally fall to earth
Burning their epitaphs in the sky

Spring's pubescent boil
Plateaus into a low Summer simmer
Languishes into Fall
Even water hardens in Winter

216

Fall of the Fox
11012019

It's Fall
The leaves are changing
Red, orange and yellow
Brown, to the ground

"GET ON THE GROUND!"
"STOP RESISTING!"

Growth beds down
Another tree ring complete
Wishing for the sun to come
The cold cuts through

A fox J-walks through the sleeping wood
Coyotes come to defend their territory
He sneers at them, walking on
They encroach to coax his rebuttal
He scoffs at their display of power

Leaves crunch beneath my feet
Concrete crunches under my face
Serpentine steel teeth zip shut
Cutting the circulation to my hands

My wallet, keys, a pen, and some change sit on top of the trunk in front of me
"Do you have anything else in your pockets?"
My hands are tied
"You're the one searching. You tell me."

A hand on my head clears the door frame
You can't sit with your back against the seat when your hands are cuffed behind you
Much less fasten a seat belt
Freshly wiped vinyl is slippery
Plastic plating makes it easy to clean-up fluids
The cage between me and them foreshadows the bars to come

Trees overcrowd each other
Fighting for sunlight and nutrients
Some won't last the winter
When the snow melts, they'll stay brown
White aspens are connected under the dirt

They snicker to each other under a parking lot lamp
Taunting their prey before the sun exposes them

Standing before the precinct doors
"Are you sure there's no weapons on you? Anything beyond this door is grounds for smuggling"
I shrug an indignant affirmation
The doors close behind us
A coyote's claw sneaks into my pocket to reveal a pocketknife
An afterthought from incredulous reeling
"Look what we have here…" a dark smile bares white teeth

"You have to plead 'no contest'.
Their cameras were off, no witnesses. It's their word against yours."
Resisting territorial entanglement with violence
Battery on two coyotes

I spend my summer stores before winter matures
Every step will now be accorded and accounted for
Coyotes eagerly await a misstep to collect
The fox treads with intent until another tree ring's set

The leaves change
But the trees stay the same
Some will be lucky enough to make it through the cold
Some will not last the winter

Reflections on Volume X

This is it! You did great! Thanks again for reading all of this. It's pretty wild putting my story out there for the world to see. Seriously, I appreciate it. Let's button this up then, shall we?

"Black n' Red" (or *Volume X*; doesn't that sound and look so cool? I think it's cool) sees me coming more into my own. I turned 28 in 2019. My spirit was less restless because I found security and direction from fulfilling a purpose. I advanced at Open Sky and moved up in seniorhood as a guide, refreshing a whole new wave of self-doubt to work through in a new position where I was solely responsible for an entire team of people in the mountainous backcountry or desert canyonlands. My friend from guide orientation that I went to Mexico with became another brother to me. I made a load of friends, and we went on regular adventures. We worked eight days straight and had six days off, plus a shift off every four or five shifts worked. I, however, worked eight shifts in a row before Mexico, then worked eleven shifts in a row. In the industry, this is basically suicide. I was still shaking those grinding habits before I realized that I'd made my goal of becoming a wilderness therapy guide and I didn't need to subject myself to that anymore.

I started taking more time off, buying massages and spa soaks, going to therapy, going camping, and I drank responsibly at parties (my body no longer allowed me to drink like I had in the past). I went on dozens of camping, rafting, mountain biking, and rock-climbing trips with friends. I attended rager parties in the woods and experienced and experimented with new things. Girls came and went, and I saw my longest-brother-from-another-mother get married. My best friend from Open Sky left to find himself and returned, still searching.

Daosim made its first appearance in my life one morning in the field in the form of a Pocket Tao Te Ching translated by Stephen Mitchell. I had no idea what importance it would come to hold for me. I was struck by its elegant wisdom and uncanny reflection of my rigidity. I would soon find myself ordering books faster than I could read them, faster than they could arrive at my door, inescapably immersed in varied translations and carrying them with me the same way you can't seem to bring yourself to throw way that twist-tie from the loaf of bread you finished, so you throw it in that one drawer in your kitchen, certain it will be your Godsend in your unforeseeable time of need.

I saw a significant upturn in my writing ability. *Heredity of Kairos* was the first poem I took several months to write, and I began to put my creativity to subjects notably more positive. This final chapter covers such a longer span of time due to things being so agreeable and having so little to process through writing. Oddly enough, I also desired to develop a more "professional, neat, organized" journal which might reinforce the same in my heart and mind.

I identified some specific negative and positive core beliefs and how to work with them. I received feedback every week in the field about how I was showing up, and I consolidated that so I could focus on areas to improve on little by little. I hit and broke through a second wall in guiding, then hit another one and drove to Joshua Tree for a near-identical simulation of the Pacific Tropics for orientation with Pacific Quest. For the first time in my life, I turned down a job because I believed myself to be worth more, and I continued guiding at Open Sky.

Oh, yeah…AND I WROTE THIS GODDAMN BOOK!

Welp, that about brings us up to speed! The rest is ongoing. So…that's it. You're free to go.

...don't make it awkward...

...look, honestly, there is more but the book's gotta end somewhere. If you really want more there's a little afterword about putting this whole thing together and how it's felt; aside from that, this is all I've got (for now). Keep an eye out for future brainzooka-soulspells from yours truly.

I'm currently sitting at a very old wooden table in a brick-face room in the Smiley Building in Durango, Colorado. There's a Diebold wall safe to my left, a whiteboard to my right, and I'm surrounded by my journals and a copy of this manuscript. EDM music is blowing and sucking my eardrums through headphones. This is where I leave you. I have a pajama party to attend. Thanks for coming!

More to come//

.vide te mox.

//Putting a book together for the first time of nearly every [notable] thing I've written from the past 1.1 decades//11 years//124 months//535 weeks//3,745 days//89,898 hours was a two-year process. It's been incredible to dig through journals and scattered trails of notes to reflect on who I have been and who I am becoming. I started writing my life down not knowing where I was going, not that it necessarily gave me any answers, but now I have the questions written down as they came. I'm figuring it out as I go—like the anyone else—but I'm finding that the best lessons are the ones we never intended. I hope reading some of this, sparks some of that for you. It's never too late.

Thank you to everyone whose played a part in my meanderings and those I have yet to meet.

The journey of a thousand miles begins with a single step//
//Tao Te Ching |64|

Write a creative sentence about what's inside or outside of you//
//Create a poem

Write a few thoughts about your day, or week, or month, or year//
//Start a journal

Write a letter to your past or future self//
//Engage your inner dialogue

Document your life and put it all together//
//Publish a book

Monday//11112019//11:11 AM

About the Author//

//Constantine was born in
St. Petersburg, Florida and raised by his mother and his aunt,
with the help of several formative programs: Cub Scouts, Boy
Scouts, Venture Crew, and Sea Scouts. He spent 3 years as the
front man for a Tampa ska/punk band: H1N1. After overcoming
blind rebellion against "the system," he attended St. Petersburg
College for his Associate of Arts, followed by New College of
Florida for his Bachelor of Arts in Psychology.

He made his initial escape to Colorado in 2015—
degrees in-hand—in search of his independence,
dedicating a year of service to City Year Denver of
AmeriCorps. There, he discovered a new passion and
direction in life: wilderness therapy. He pursued his
first and only dream and vision in life with ferocity to
become a field guide with Open Sky Wilderness
Therapy, completing nearly 550 days in the field.

He enjoys writing,
tea,
cooking,
brooding,
dancing,
yoga,
astronomy,
reprehensibly long walks,
movies,
being outdoors,
etc. & suchforth//